The
Speed Reading
Book

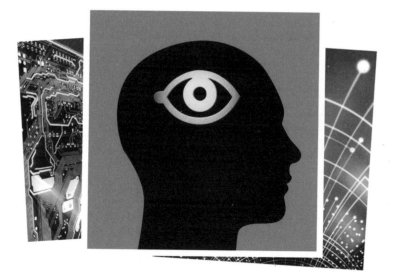

The
Speed Reading
Book
Read more, learn more, achieve more

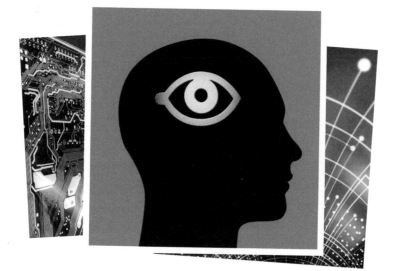

Tony Buzan™

Consultant Editor, James Harrison

Special Consultant, Anne Jones, World Speed
Reading Champion

PEARSON

Harlow, England • London • New York • Boston • San Francisco • Toronto • Sydney • Singapore • Hong Kong
Tokyo • Seoul • Taipei • New Delhi • Cape Town • Madrid • Mexico City • Amsterdam • Munich • Paris • Milan

Published by BBC Active, an imprint of Educational Publishers LLP, part of the
Pearson Education Group, Edinburgh Gate, Harlow, Essex, CM20 2JE, England.

First published in Great Britain in 2010

ISBN: 978-1-4066-4429-6

British Library Cataloguing-in-Publication Data
A catalogue record for this book is available from the British Library

Library of Congress Cataloging-in-Publication Data
A catalog record for this book is available from the Library of Congress

10 9 8 7 6 5 4 3 2 1
13 12 11 10 09

Text design by Design Deluxe
Typeset in 9.5 Swis721 Lt BT by 30
Printed and bound in Great Britain by Ashford Colour Press Ltd, Gosport, Hants

The publisher's policy is to use paper manufactured from sustainable forests.

To my dear, dear mum, who so lovingly and so caringly introduced me to the beauty and power of the word; the beauty and power of the mind.

Contents

Part 4 Mastermind your speed reading skills 153

Foreword

I read *The Speed Reading Book* for the first time in 1996. If anyone had told me then that, years later, I would be writing the foreword for a new edition of it, I would not have believed it.

Reading the first page for the first time, I knew very little about speed reading and I was doubtful about whether I could do it. I need not have worried. Just over a year later, I had won my first world championship and I was speed reading books with ease, at over 1000 words per minute. Back in 1996, I could never, even in my wildest dreams, have imagined what would happen in 2007 with *Harry Potter and the Deathly Hallows*. I was asked to speed read this extraordinary book when it was released and was interviewed about it by press and television. The speed – 4251 words per minute – was my fastest yet.

As you embark on your speed reading adventure, arm yourself with two things: a deep curiosity about what your brain can achieve when you push it beyond what you think is possible; and a book that you really, really want to read. Practise with your chosen book, as well as with this one. How you learn a new skill is important. Make a link to fun and enjoyment right from the start. I did. I used to find a book that I wanted to read and challenge myself to read it in a fast time. I would guess how long it would take me and discover whether I was right. The benefit of learning this way is the relaxed concentration you will achieve whenever you speed read subsequently.

Find out what happens when you read very fast. As a Star Trek fan, I think it is the nearest we can get to a 'mind meld' with the author (unless, of course, we have pointed ears and come from the planet Vulcan). All our attention is in the reading process and we are completely in the moment and totally absorbed by it. It is very Zen-like. I find that I remember information that I have read at fast speeds better than stuff I have read slowly. My mind does not have time to wander off.

This book will give you all the information you need to become a good speed reader. If you would like to become a great one, read Tony Buzan's books on Mind Maps and memory (which form part of this revised and updated *Mind Set* series) as well. Learn how to Mind Map books and articles – it trains the brain to identify key concepts quickly and helps to develop memory skills. Being able to create mental imagery as you read is the key to improving recall.

The Speed Reading Book is the classic book on speed reading. Turn the pages and you will accelerate your reading speed, while improving comprehension and memory. This combination delivers a competitive edge for business and a profound synthesis for academic study. It is where I started – page 1, to be precise.

Anne Jones
Six-times winner of the World Speed Reading Championship
Mind Sports Olympiad record-holder
www.speedyreader.co.uk

Acknowledgements

My heart- and mind-felt thanks to the following who made this book possible: Anne Jones for her kind foreword and inspiring speed read of over 4000 words a minute *with* comprehension and enjoyment of *Harry Potter*! The entire Folley family for providing me with the glorious surroundings in which to complete the original manuscript; Caro and Peter Ayre for providing the sanctuary of Greenham Hall where much of the early research was completed; Robyn Pontynen of Lizard Island, Australia, who similarly provided me with care and sustenance during the gestation period; and The Brain Trust and all members of the Brain Clubs for their commitment to the global goal of Mental Literacy and, in particular, to the concept of speed reading.

Bringing *The Speed Reading Book* into the twenty-first century, 'the century of the Brain', has been a global team effort, and I would like to extend my heartfelt appreciation to the entire network of Buzan Centres International now well and truly established – and growing. Thank you to all the Buzan Master Trainers and Licensed Instructors from Buzan World, including Masanori Kanda, Mikiko Chickada Kawase, Ken Ito and Shiro Kobayashi in Japan; Henry Toi and Eric Cheung; Thum Cheng Cheong and the Buzan Asia team in Singapore; Jorge O. Castañeda, President, Buzan Latin America; Bill Jarrard and Jennifer Goddard at Buzan Centre Australia/NZ; and Hilde Jaspaert at Buzan Europe.

Thank you also to Brian Lee for being a friend and stalwart in helping me to bring the *Mind Set* series to the public; and to Phil Chambers, World Mind Mapping Champion and Senior Buzan Licensed Instructor, for his superb Mind Map creations and for his tireless backroom input.

My thanks also to my 'home team' at Buzan HQ, including Anne Reynolds, Suzi Rockett and Jenny Redman for their superb logistical support and effort.

At Pearson, the publishers, I would like to thank Richard Stagg, Director, who was a prime figure in the launching of this project; and to add my profound thanks to Samantha Jackson, my cherished commissioning editor, for her total commitment to *The Speed Reading Book* throughout its long gestation; also to her team in Harlow, Caroline Jordan, Colette Holden and Melanie Carter. My thanks would not be complete without acknowledgement to James Harrison, my independent consultant editor, for helping to shape, structure and nail everything together.

Finally, my acknowledgements to all those speed readers and educators who enthusiastically provided speed reading stories and tests, both for the first edition and this revised and updated edition, and who for reasons of space I have either omitted to thank or been unable to include.

Lastly, dear reader, a special thanks to you for joining the growing global community of speed readers. PLEASE do contact me with your speed reading-related stories and ideas for possible inclusion in the next edition of *The Speed Reading Book* at tony.buzan@buzanworld.com.

Introduction

Reading is to the mind as aerobic training is to the body.

There has never been a better time to learn and apply the rescue remedy of speed reading. The technique will aid you to supercharge your mind's eye and drastically reduce the time taken to read a typical 250-page book – from nearly ten and a half hours to 60 minutes! Follow the speed reading course and you will be able to scan, sift, sort and retain the terabytes of information travelling along the World Wide Web's superhighway, not to mention manage the mountainous heaps of hard facts from all kinds of printed media. Along with Mind Maps and other memory-boosting techniques, mastering speed reading will greatly enhance your study and work skills.

How were you taught to read?

Can you remember by which method you were taught to read? Was it the phonic method, or the look–say method, or a combination of both?

The phonic method

The phonic method first introduces the child to the ordinary alphabet from A to Z, and then introduces the sound of each letter so that 'a' becomes 'ah', 'b' becomes 'buh', and so on. The child is then introduced to the letters and sounds in the context of words. Thus, 'the cat' will first be read 'tuh-heh-eh kuh-ah-tuh' (not 'see-aye-tee', etc.), until the teacher has moulded the word into its proper form. When the child has learnt to make the correct sounds (vocalises properly), he or she is told to read silently. This last stage often takes a long time, and many children and even adults never get past the stage of moving their lips while reading. Those who do get past this stage may nevertheless still be vocalising to themselves. That is to say, as they read, they are consciously aware of the sound of each word. This is called sub-vocalisation.

The look–say method of teaching children to read also relies on a word or verbal response. The child is shown a picture (for example, a cow) with the word that represents the object printed clearly beneath it, thus: 'cow'. The teacher then asks the child for the correct response. If the incorrect answer is given (for example, 'elephant'), the teacher guides the child to the correct response and then moves on to the next word. When the child has reached a reasonable level of proficiency, he or she will be in a position similar to the child who has been taught by the phonic method: able to read, still vocalising and told to read silently.

What is real literacy?

Once the child is able to recognise words and to read silently, it is generally assumed that he or she has learnt to read and is therefore literate. From the age of five to seven years onwards, very little further instruction is given, as it is believed that, once the skill of reading has been learnt, the child needs only to apply it.

Nothing could be further from the truth: for what has in fact been taught is the very first *stage* of reading. Leaving the child in this state, in which he or she remains until adulthood, is very much like assuming that, once a baby has learnt to crawl, the process of locomotion is complete. Yet the worlds of walking, running, dancing and related activities have all been left unexplored. The same applies to reading. We have been left stranded on the floor; now it is time to learn to walk, run and dance!

Tony's speed reading journey

When I was 14, my class was given a battery of tests to measure our mental skills. Among them was a speed reading test. A few weeks later we were given our results, and I found that I had scored an average of 213 words per minute (wpm). My first reaction was elation, because 213 sounded like a lot. However, my joy did not last long, for our teacher soon explained that the fastest student in the class had scored 314 wpm – just over 100 wpm faster than my score.

This demoralising piece of news was to change my life: as soon as the class ended, I rushed up to the teacher and asked him how I could improve my speed. He answered that there was no way of doing so, and that your reading speed, like your IQ, your adult height and the colour of your eyes, was fundamentally unchangeable.

This did not quite ring true to me. Why? I had just started a vigorous physical training programme and had noticed, within a few weeks, dramatic changes in nearly every muscle of my body. If knowing the right exercises had enabled me to bring about such physical transformation, why shouldn't the appropriate visual and mental exercises allow me to change my reading speed, comprehension and memory of what I had read?

These questions launched me on a search that soon had me cracking the 400 wpm barrier and eventually reading comfortably at speeds of over 1000 wpm. Through these investigations, I realised that, on all levels, *reading is to the mind as aerobic training is to the body.*

Where did it all begin? The development of speed reading

Speed reading originated at the beginning of the twentieth century, when the publication explosion swamped readers with more than they could possibly handle at normal reading rates. Most early courses, however, were based on information from a rather unexpected source – the Royal Air Force.

During the First World War, air force tacticians had found that, when flying, a number of pilots were unable to distinguish planes seen at a distance. In the life-and-death situation of air combat, this was obviously a serious disadvantage, and the tacticians set about finding a remedy. They developed a machine called a tachistoscope, which flashes images for varying short spaces of time on a large screen. They started by flashing fairly large pictures of friendly and enemy aircraft at very slow exposures and then gradually shortened the exposure, while decreasing the size and changing the angle of the image seen. To their surprise, they found that, with training, the average person was able to distinguish almost speck-like representations of different planes when the images had been flashed on the screen for only a five-hundredth of a second.

Reasoning that, if the eyes could see at this incredible speed, then reading speeds could be dramatically improved, they decided to transfer this information to reading. Using exactly the same device, they first flashed one word in large type for as long as five seconds on a screen, gradually reducing the size of the word and shortening the length of each flash. Eventually they were flashing four words simultaneously on a screen for a five-hundredth of a second, and the subjects were still able to read them.

As a consequence of these findings, most speed reading courses have been based on this flash-card or tachistoscopic training (also known as still-screen training).

Reading speed (wpm)

Individual
progress –
tachistoscope
trained

Reading speed (wpm)

Individual
progress –
properly
trained

Average
progress –
tachistoscope
trained

Figure I.1 (a) tachistoscopic graph; (b) measuring the relative effectiveness of tachistoscopic training against natural reading speeds.

The tachistoscopic trainers usually measured the student's progress with a graph graded in units of ten from 100 to 400 words per minute (Figure I.1). With regular training, most people were able to climb from an average of 200 words per minute to an average of 400 per minute, precisely the difference between the junior school pupil and the postgraduate student.

However, the successful tachistoscopic students reported a general dissatisfaction with their results after a few weeks of 'postgraduate reading'. Most reported that, shortly after their course had finished, their reading speed once again sank to its previous level. Again, this is very similar to the reversion to the norm of the standard adult reader.

On average, with this method, an individual's speed rises from 200 words to 400 wpm. At first this sounds wonderful: a doubling of reading speed. However, if you look at the mathematics, it becomes clear that something is drastically amiss. If the eye is able to recognise images (for example, a plane or a word) in a five-hundredth of a second, then the expected reading speed in a minute would be 60 seconds × 500 words per second = 30,000 (or a short book) in a minute! Where have the other 29,600 words gone? Or to put it another way, if the normal range of reading ability is from roughly 200 to 400 wpm and most people operate at the lower end of this range, then a typical 250-page book, with about 500 words per page, would take nearly ten and a half hours to read. The increased reading ability observed during the tachisto-scopic courses in fact had little to do with the training. It was due more to the students being highly motivated over a period of weeks and thus being able to reach the top of their normal range.

Although not a comprehensive approach to speed reading, the tachistoscope technique became useful as one part of a basic training kit, and the average speed for a good speed reader began to nudge the next great barrier – 1000 wpm. Fuelled by stories of the speed reading exploits of such public figures as US President John F. Kennedy and the interest shown by President Jimmy Carter, the dynamic reading schools flourished and spawned many variants. Among these was photo-reading, which simply focused on the ability of the eye to 'photograph' larger areas of print than normal.

Speed reading world record-holders

Speed reading tests are based primarily on the reading of novels. The reader has to read an entire novel as fast as possible, subsequently giving a speech to people who have already read the novel in depth. The speech has to include knowledgeable comments about all the following main areas: characters, setting, plot, philosophy, symbolism, language level, literary style, metaphor, themes, and historical context. Among the early 'hall of fame' speed readers were Michael J. Gelb from the USA, with a speed of 1805 wpm, and Mithymna Corke from the Netherlands, who broke the 2000 wpm barrier with 2100. But Corke's compatriot Kjetill Gunnarson broke the 3000 wpm barrier with 3050, and Sean Adam from the USA came close to 4000 wpm with a tantalising 3850. In 2007 the six times world champion speed reader Anne Jones read *Harry Potter and the Deathly Hallows* at Borders, Charing Cross Road, London in a record-breaking 47 minutes and 1 second – making an astonishing 4251 wpm. She then reviewed the book for the *Independent* and for Sky TV. (Anne has very generously contributed her Championship speed reading experience to this book, including the contribution of her foreword.)

If you are interested in joining this speed reading elite, read this book thoroughly, make sure you practise all the exercises, join the Brain Club worldwide, send me your top reading speed to date, and make sure you enter the World Speed Reading Championships (for more information, visit www.worldspeedreadingcouncil.com).

Your speed reading potential

Your own potential to improve your reading speed to at least double your present rate, and eventually to reach 1000 wpm, is identical to all those in the world's current top ten. Each one of them was a reader who, like you and I, was initially dissatisfied with his or her normal reading speed and decided to put time and effort into developing this most powerful of human skills. *The Speed Reading Book* gives you the perfect opportunity to follow in their eye-steps. It is the result of over 50 years of practice and research in the field.

Going back to my teenage years, by learning about the miracle of my eyes and the extraordinary capacity of my brain, I increased my speed, comprehension and memory; I also found myself able to think faster and more creatively, to make better notes, to pass exams with relative ease, to study more successfully, and to save days, weeks and even months of my time.

In *The Speed Reading Book* you will be introduced to exercises that allow you to develop precisely those skills inherent in both your eyes and your brain, enabling you to combine the two into a single tool that will make you an intellectual powerhouse. Its pages contain the essential secrets I learnt during my speed reading journey. I hope you find *your* journey exciting, and benefit as much from these mental literacy techniques as I have done. If you follow up my speed reading programme with regular practice, then 1000–2000 wpm with good comprehension is certainly attainable. This would mean that you could read this 250-page book in an hour! Now read on to find out how.

Getting the most from *The Speed Reading Book*

This book has six main purposes:

1 To improve your reading speed dramatically

2 To improve and maintain your comprehension

3 To increase your understanding of the function of your eyes and your brain, in order to help you use them far more effectively while reading and studying, and also to use them more effectively in your everyday personal and professional life

4 To help you improve your vocabulary and general knowledge

5 To save you time

6 To give you confidence.

How to use this book

This book works like a course manual, starting with a self-assessment of your current reading speed and comprehension levels and then moving progressively, with a series of self-tests and exercises, through a range of guided reading and masterminding vocabulary techniques to strengthen your eye/brain system and to accelerate your reading speed. Common reading problems, from distractions to dyslexia, are highlighted and tackled; and specific areas of reading and research, including newspapers and magazines, and how to deal with the information explosion emanating from computer screens, are also flagged up. You will also be shown how to apply speed reading techniques to literature and poetry. At the back of the book you will find the self-test answers, your progress chart and graph, an index, and information on the World Speed Reading Council, the Speed Reading Championship and Brain Club websites.

The self-tests

Seven of the chapters in *The Speed Reading Book* contain a graded series of articles and selected readings that will give you a continuing indication of your progress. The self-tests at the beginning of the book are designed to increase your reading speed, those in the middle will develop your powers of perception and vocabulary, and those at the end will enable you to achieve your full speed reading potential. Some of these readings deal with the history and theory of the major areas of human knowledge; others are articles on research into learning and the brain. By the time you finish the book you will therefore have increased your reading speed, improved your comprehension, and heightened your critical and appreciative abilities; you will also have gained a wider knowledge of yourself and the universe around you. These self-tests are:

1 The intelligence war – at the front with brain training (see page 22)

2 Challenge your memory (see page 49)

3 Animal intelligence (see page 68)

4 Are we alone in the universe? Extra-terrestrial intelligences (see page 115)

5 Baby brain (see page 127)

6 Your brain – the enchanted loom (see page 189)

7 Embrace creativity and watch your profits grow! (see page 206).

The exercises

You will also have workouts with special exercises designed to enhance your visual perception, mental awareness, critical faculties and the power of your vocabulary. Like muscle-building exercises, many of these exercises will benefit you even more if you repeat them several times. The first warm-up starts below.

How to speed read The Speed Reading Book

The Speed Reading Book is a one-week, two-week, three-week or four-week course, depending on how speedily you wish to accomplish your goals. Read the next few paragraphs, and then draw up your study plans.

1 Go through the table of contents thoroughly, mapping out the territory you wish to cover.

2 Roughly plan the time period you will devote to each division of the book, finishing with a general outline in your mind's eye of both the content and your programme of study. This should take only a few minutes.

3 Quickly browse through the entire book, familiarise yourself with the different divisions, and start filling in your mental picture of the 'continent' of the book and your goals.

4 Decide whether you wish to complete a chapter a day, or two or three chapters a day, or whether you wish to vary your pace.

5 Once you have made these decisions, record your study plan in your diary, marking the date on which you will begin and the date on which you will finish the book. When you are calculating this, bear in mind that each chapter is on average only ten pages long and that most of the exercises will be easy for you to accomplish.

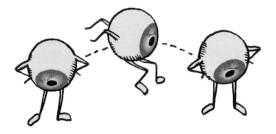

Warm-up Q&A

Exploring your speeds

You are about to embark on one of the most exciting journeys of your life – to stimulate your thinking about reading and speed reading, follow the quiz on reading habits and skills. Answer yes or no for each of the 20 questions, then check your results on page 11.

1 Speeds of over 1000 words per minute are possible. *Yes/No*

2 For better comprehension, you should read slowly and carefully. *Yes/No*

3 Word-for-word reading helps comprehension. *Yes/No*

4 Sub-vocalisation is a reading habit that slows you down and should be reduced or eliminated. *Yes/No*

5 You should endeavour to understand 100 per cent of what you read. *Yes/No*

6 You should attempt to remember 100 per cent of what you read. *Yes/No*

7 Your eye should sweep in a continuous flowing movement along the line as it reads. *Yes/No*

8 When you miss something while reading, you should skip back to make sure you understand it before you move on. *Yes/No*

9 Reading with your finger on the page slows you down and should be eliminated with training. *Yes/No*

10 When you encounter problems of comprehension and understanding in the text, you should work them out before moving on to the following text in order to guarantee your ongoing comprehension. *Yes/No*

11 A good or important book should be read page by page, never reading page 20 until you have read page 19, and certainly not reading the end before you have completed the beginning. *Yes/No*

12 Skipping words is a lazy habit and should be eliminated. *Yes/No*

13 When you come to important items in a text, you
    should note them in order to improve your memory. *Yes/No*

14 Your level of motivation does not affect the fundamental
    ways in which your eyes communicate with your brain
    and does not affect your reading speed. *Yes/No*

15 Your notes should always be in a neat, ordered and
    structured form – mainly sentences and organised
    lists of the information you have read. *Yes/No*

16 When you come to a word that you do not understand,
    you should have a dictionary close at hand so that
    you can look it up immediately. *Yes/No*

17 One of the dangers of reading faster is that your
    comprehension is reduced. *Yes/No*

18 We all read, by definition, at a natural reading speed. *Yes/No*

19 For novels and poetry, slower reading speeds are
    important in order to appreciate the meaning of the
    information and the rhythm of the language. *Yes/No*

20 You will only truly be able to understand what your
    eyes focus clearly on. *Yes/No*

Answers to speed reading warm-up

If you have answered only one of these questions with a 'yes', then you
are nearly ready to become one of our speed reading teachers. And
that one question was the first – speeds of 1000 wpm are possible.

All the other questions should have been answered with a
resounding 'no'. These remaining 19 questions covered the full
range of current misconceptions about reading.

If you believe these false assumptions, then not only are you believing in something that is not true but also you are believing in
something that will actively make your reading habits progressively
worse, your reading speed progressively slower, and your comprehension and understanding progressively more difficult and unsatisfactory.

As you progress through *The Speed Reading Book*, these false assumptions will be knocked down one by one, finally leaving you with a clear path on which you can move towards the accomplishment of your own speed reading goals.

The first chapter of this book will help you check your current normal speed reading and comprehension levels. It is not a speed reading 'test'; it forms the foundation from which you can improve your speed reading skills in leaps and bounds.

Definition is the companion of **clarity**; **clarity** is the guide to **your goals**.

Part 1

Discover and develop your speed reading skills

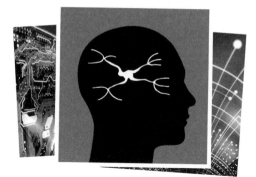

This section explains the eye/brain process we call 'reading' and breaks it down to pinpoint the ways we can improve on it – and literally speed it up. The first of a series of self-tests helps you explore your current reading speed and normal comprehension so you know exactly where you are now. The next chapters show you how to gain control of those amazing eyes of yours so you can increase immediately your reading speed and improve your comprehension.

You will also learn techniques that will help you to guide your eyes more effectively on the page, to develop advanced skimming and scanning skills, and to arrange your environment in a way that actually helps your eyes and brain read faster. To aid your speed reading and comprehension, you will be given exercises and speed reading tests that enable you to strengthen the muscle of your eye/brain system and continue to accelerate your reading speed.

Reading: a new revolutionary definition

Before you start learning the skills of speed reading, ask yourself this simple question: *what is reading?* Write your definition in the space below:

_____

_____

_____

Now compare your answer with these common definitions:

● Reading is understanding what the author intended.

● Reading is taking in the written word.

● Reading is the assimilation of information.

Each of these standard definitions covers only a part of the process. An accurate definition of reading must include the full range of reading skills.

What is reading? A new definition

Reading is a seven-part process comprising the following steps (see Figure 1.1):

1 **Recognition**: you have to be able to recognise the language, and whatever language you learn it's the same. It doesn't matter where you come from, what age, sex, race or educational level you are at – the process for the brain is to recognise the symbols, whether it's the phonic or look–say system; getting the symbols into the brain.

2 How do the symbols get in? That is **assimilation**. It is more complex. It relates to your posture, health, general physical condition, and primarily your eye and how your brain uses it. You need to know how your eye functions and what actually goes on in order to work it; and yet nobody is taught this.

3 Now you have to **compherend** it; this is called 'intra-integration' (intra meaning 'within') or connecting bits of information – the interconnection of the information within the text to itself.

4 **Understanding** is different from comprehension. Once you have comprehended, you then can integrate that information with the outside world – 'extra-integration', connecting the book to the outside universe. A very different process from branch 3 (which is getting the book totally connected to itself in your head). This branch is getting the book completely related to other areas of knowledge.

5 Now you have learnt to store – to retain – the information. **Retention** is storing in your filing cabinet, your archive.

6 **Recall** is fishing for the information to hook it out – and you have to know how to do that. This is generally otherwise known as memory. Don't confuse retention and recall. Don't say, 'I have a terrible memory'; it's not true. You have a wonderful memory but you are mismanaging it. You are confusing retention and recall. For most people, memory is recall, the second stage of memory.

7 Why recall? Why read in the first place? You want to apply and **communicate** the knowledge you have acquired in order to create from it, to learn from it, and to build for life long future learning.

Assimilation is all about how we get that information into our heads – and that is where all the facets of speed reading come into play.

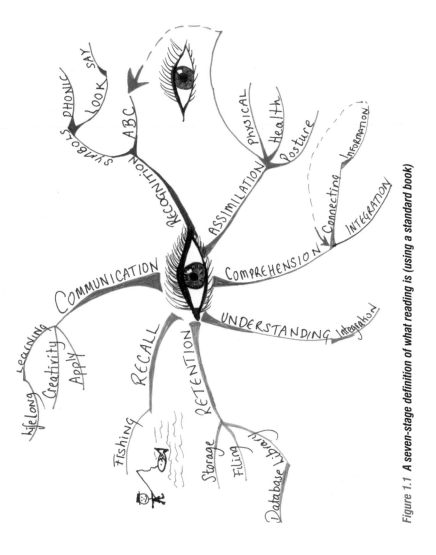

Figure 1.1 A seven-stage definition of what reading is (using a standard book)

1 *Recognition – your knowledge of the alphabetic symbols. This step takes place before physical reading begins.*
2 *Assimilation – the physical process by which light is reflected from the word, received by your eye, and then transmitted, via your optic nerve, to your brain.*
3 *Comprehension – I also call this equivalent of basic comprehension intra-integration, referring to the linking of all parts of the information being read with all other appropriate parts.*
4 *Understanding – the process by which you bring all of your previous knowledge to what you read, making appropriate connections, analysing, criticising, appreciating, selecting and rejecting. I also call this extra-integration.*
5 *Retention – the basic storage of information. Many readers will have experienced entering an examination room, storing most of the required information during the two-hour period and recalling it only as they leave. Storage, then, is not enough and must be accompanied by recall.*
6 *Recall – the ability to get back out of storage that which is needed, preferably when it is needed.*
7 *Communication – the use to which the information is put immediately or eventually. Communication includes written, keyed in, spoken and representational (e.g. art, dance and other forms of creative expression) communication.*

Reading also includes that vitally important and often neglected human function, *thinking*. Thinking is your ongoing intra- and extra-integration.

In the light of this *real* definition, it can be seen that the top 30 common reading and learning problems outlined in the box below can all be dealt with easily by the reader who has learned to *recognise* the word and to *assimilate, comprehend, understand, retain, recall* and *communicate*.

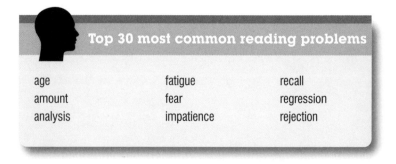

Top 30 most common reading problems

age	fatigue	recall
amount	fear	regression
analysis	impatience	rejection

appreciation	interest	retention
back-skipping	laziness	selection
boredom	legibility	speed
comprehension	literary style	stimulation
concentration	noting	sub-vocalisation
criticism	motivation	surroundings
distraction	organisation	time

Reading is a multi-level process. Every level must be developed if you are to become an effective speed reader.

Before you embark on the first self-test below, rank the seven steps in order, giving the ranking 1 to the step you feel it is most important for you to develop:

Recognise

Assimilate

Comprehend

Understand

Retain

Recall

Communicate.

From the list of reading problems, identify the ones you have and are going to eliminate.

Now that you comprehend what the act of reading actually entails, you are ready to try your first test. In any learning or self-improvement situation, it is essential to find the true base from which you start. Only an accurate assessment of where you are positioned at present, whatever that position is, will form a solid foundation from which you can springboard to your ultimate goal.

Self-testing: where are you now?

Check your normal reading speed and comprehension.

This two-part test is exactly the opposite of all the other tests you will attempt in *The Speed Reading Book* because this is not a speed reading test, instead it is a test to calculate your current speed in order to judge accurately the progress you make throughout the book.

Your comprehension level will also be tested at the end with 15 multiple-choice and true/false questions. When reading the passage, *don't* go for very high or very low levels of comprehension; go for *exactly* the same kind of comprehension you would normally expect to get when reading this type of material.

Don't worry about getting low scores in either speed or comprehension. Remember that this book has been written for people who want to improve their reading skills and that low initial scores are not only common, they are expected.

So, no dashing along for higher-than-usual speeds, no plodding for super comprehension scores, and no worrying about your result.

Have your watch by your side, and do your reading privately (someone timing you or watching you inevitably interferes with your comprehension and tends to make some people read more hurriedly or more slowly than usual).

When you have reached the end of the article, immediately check your watch and calculate your speed. Full instructions will be given on how to do this.

Prepare yourself, and start a normal reading of the following passage now.

SELF-TEST 1

The intelligence war – at the front with brain training

New world trends
Stock market analysts watch, like hawks, ten individuals in Silicon Valley. When there is even a hint that one might move from Company A to Company B, the world's stock markets shift.

The English Manpower Services Commission has published a survey in which it was noted that, of the top 10 per cent of British companies, 80 per cent invested considerable money and time in training; in the bottom 10 per cent of companies, no money or time was invested.

In Minnesota, the Plato Computer Education Project has already raised the thinking and academic performance levels of 200,000 pupils.

In the armed forces of an increasing number of countries, mental martial arts are becoming as important as physical combat skills.

National Olympic squads are devoting as much as 80 per cent of their training time to the development of positive mind set, mental stamina and visualisation.

In the Fortune 500 (the 500 top-earning US companies), the top five computer companies alone have spent over a billion dollars on educating their employees, and the development of intellectual capital has become the main priority, including the development of the world's most powerful currency – the currency of intelligence.

In Caracas, Dr Luis Alberto Machado became the first person to be given a government portfolio as Minister of Intelligence, with a political mandate to increase the mental power of the nation.

We are witnessing a quantum leap in human evolution – the awareness by intelligence of itself, and the concomitant awareness that this intelligence can be nurtured to astounding advantage.

This encouraging news must be considered in the context of the most significant problem areas as defined by the business community. Over the past 20 years over 100,000 people from each of the five major continents have been polled. The top 20 areas commonly mentioned as requiring improvement are:

1 Reading speed
2 Reading comprehension
3 General study skills
4 Handling the information explosion
5 Memory
6 Concentration
7 Oral communication skills
8 Written communication skills
9 Creative thinking
10 Planning

11 Note-taking

12 Problem analysis

13 Problem-solving

14 Motivation

15 Analytical thinking

16 Prioritising

17 Time management

18 Assimilation of information

19 Getting started (procrastination)

20 Mental ability declining with age.

With the aid of modern research on the functioning of the brain, each of these problems can be tackled with relative ease. This research covers:

- The functions of the left and right cortex
- Mind Maps
- Super-speed and range reading/intellectual commando units
- Mnemonic techniques
- Memory loss after learning
- The brain cell
- Mental abilities and ageing.

The functions of the left and right cortex

It has now become common knowledge that the left and right cortical structures of the brain tend to deal with different intellectual functions. The left cortex primarily handles logic, words, numbers, sequence, analysis, linearity and listing, while the right cortex processes rhythm, colour, imagination, daydreaming, spatial relationships and dimension.

What has recently been realised is that the left cortex is not the 'academic' side and the right cortex the 'creative, intuitive, emotional' side. We now know from volumes of research that both sides need to be used in conjunction with each other for there to be both academic and creative success.

The Einsteins, Newtons, Cézannes and Mozarts of this world, like the great business geniuses, combined their linguistic, numerical and analytical skills with imagination and visualisation in order to produce their creative masterpieces.

Mind Maps

Using this basic knowledge of our mental functioning, it is possible to train people in order to solve each of these problem areas, often producing incremental improvements of 500 per cent.

One of the modern methods of achieving such improvements is Mind Mapping.

In traditional note-taking, whether it be for remembering information, for preparing written or oral communication, for organising your thoughts, for problem analysis, for planning or for creative thinking, the standard mode of presentation is linear, using sentences, short lists of phrases, or numerically and alphabetically ordered lists. These methods, because of their lack of colour, visual rhythm, image and spatial relationships, cauterise the brain's thinking capacities and impede each of the aforementioned mental processes.

Mind Mapping, by contrast, uses the full range of the brain's abilities, placing an image in the centre of the page in order to facilitate memorisation and the creative generation of ideas, and subsequently branching out in associative networks that mirror externally the brain's internal structures. Using this approach, you can prepare speeches in minutes rather than days; problems can be solved both more comprehensively and more rapidly; memory can be improved from absent to perfect; and creative thinkers can generate a limitless number of ideas rather than a truncated list.

Super-speed and range reading

By combining Mind Maps with new super-speed and range reading techniques (which allow speeds of well over 1000 words per minute (wpm) along with excellent comprehension, and eventual effective reading speeds of about 10,000 wpm), one can form 'intellectual commando units'.

Reading at these advanced speeds, Mind Mapping in detail the outline of the book and its chapters, and exchanging the information gathered by using advanced Mind Mapping and presentation skills, it is possible for four or more individuals to acquire, integrate, memorise and begin to apply in their professional situation four complete books' worth of new information in one day.

These techniques have been applied in the multinational organisations Nabisco and Digital Computers. In these instances, 40 and 120 senior executives respectively divided their groups into four. Each individual in each of the four sub-groups spent two hours applying speed and range reading techniques to one of the four selected business books.

When the two hours were completed, the members of each sub-group discussed among themselves their understandings, interpretations and reactions to the book. Each sub-group then chose one representative who gave a comprehensive lecture to all the members of the three other sub-groups. This process was repeated four times, and at the end of each day 40 and 120 senior executives in each company walked out of their seminar room with four complete new books' worth of information not only in their heads, but integrated, analysed and memorised.

This approach can be similarly used in family and home study situations just as effectively.

Mnemonic techniques

Mnemonic (pronounced 'nem-on-ic') or memory-enhancing techniques were originally invented by the Greeks. We now realise that these devices are soundly based on the brain's functioning and that, when applied appropriately, they can dramatically improve anyone's memory.

Mnemonic techniques require you to use the principles of association and imagination, to create dramatic, colourful, sensual and consequently unforgettable images in your mind.

The Mind Map is in fact a multidimensional mnemonic, using the brain's inbuilt functions to imprint more effectively data/information upon itself.

Using mnemonics, businesspeople have been trained to remember perfectly 40 newly introduced people, and to similarly memorise lists of over 100 products, with relevant facts and data. These techniques have been applied at the IBM Training Centre in Stockholm and have had a major impact on the success of the centre's 17-week introductory training programme. The same techniques have been used in the World Memory Championships for the past five years, especially by the eight-times world champion and record-holder Dominic O'Brien.

There is an increasing awareness that learning how to learn before any other training has been given is good business sense. This is why a number of the more progressive international organisations are now making mnemonics the obligatory front end to all their training courses. Simple calculation shows that if £1,000,000 is spent on training, and 80 per cent of that training is forgotten within two weeks, then £800,000 has been lost during that same period.

Memory loss after learning

Memory loss after learning is dramatic: after a one-hour learning period, there is a short rise in the recall of information as the brain integrates the new data. This is followed by a dramatic decline in which, after 24 hours, as much as 80 per cent of detail is lost.

The scale remains roughly the same regardless of the length of input time. Thus, a three-day course is more or less forgotten within one to two weeks of completion.

The implications are disturbing: if a multinational firm spends U$50 million per year on training and there is no appropriate reviewing programmed into the educational structure, $40 million will have been lost with incredible efficiency within a few days of that training's completion.

By gaining a simple understanding of the memory's rhythms, it is possible not only to avert this decline but also to train people in such a way as to increase the amount learnt and retained.

The brain cell

The brain cell has become the new frontier in the human search for knowledge.

We each have one hundred thousand million brain cells, and the interconnections between them can form a staggeringly large number of patterns and permutations. This number, calculated by the Russian neuroanatomist Pyotr K. Anokhin, is one followed by ten million kilometres of standard typewritten zeros!

With our inherent capacity to integrate and juggle multiple billions of bits of data, it has become apparent to those involved in brain research that adequate training of our phenomenal biocomputer (which can calculate in one second what it would take IBM's Roadrunner supercomputer – currently the world's fastest computer, costing US$133 million – 100 years to accomplish) will enormously accelerate and increase our ability to solve problems, to analyse, to prioritise, to create and to communicate.

Mental abilities and ageing

'They die!' is the usual chorus from people in response to the question 'What happens to your brain cells as they get older?' It is usually voiced with extraordinary and surprising enthusiasm.

However, one of the most delightful pieces of news from modern brain research comes from Dr Marion Diamond of the University of California, who

▶

has confirmed that there is no evidence of brain cell loss with age in normal, active and healthy brains.

On the contrary, research is now indicating that, if the brain is used and trained, there is a biological increase in its interconnective complexity, i.e. the person's intelligence is raised.

Training of people in their sixties, seventies, eighties and nineties has shown that, in every area of mental performance, statistically significant and permanent improvements can be made.

We are at the beginning of an unprecedented revolution: the quantum leap in the development of human intelligence.

On the personal front, in education and in business, information from psychological, neurophysiological and educational laboratories is being used to solve problems that hitherto were accepted as an inevitable part of the ageing process.

By applying our knowledge of the brain's separate functions, by externally reflecting our internal processes in Mind Map form, by making use of the innate elements and rhythms of memory, and by applying our knowledge of the brain cell and the possibilities for continued mental improvement throughout life, we realise that the intelligence war can indeed be won.

STOP YOUR TIMER NOW!

Length of time: _____ min

Next, calculate your reading speed in words per minute (wpm) by dividing the number of words in the passage (in this case, 1850) by the time (in minutes) you took.

$$\text{Words per minute (wpm)} = \frac{\text{number of words}}{\text{time}}$$

When you have completed your calculation, enter the number in the wpm slot at the end of this paragraph and also enter it on the progress graph and chart on pages 222–3.

Words per minute: _____

Self-test 1: Comprehension
For each question, circle either 'True' or 'False' or tick the right answer.

1 The top 80 per cent of British companies invest considerable
   money and time in training.   True/False
2 National Olympic squads are devoting how much of their training time to
   the development of positive mind set, mental stamina and visualisation?
   (a) 20 per cent
   (b) 30 per cent
   (c) 40 per cent
   (d) 80 per cent
3 The first person to be given a government portfolio as Minister of
   Intelligence was:
   (a) Dr Marion Diamond
   (b) Dr Luis Alberto Machado
   (c) Dominic O'Brien
   (d) Plato
4 Number is mainly a left-cortex function.   True/False
5 The Einsteins, Newtons, Cézannes and Mozarts of this world
   were successful because they primarily combined:
   (a) number with logic
   (b) words with analysis
   (c) colour with rhythm
   (d) analysis with imagination
6 In Mind Mapping, you:
   (a) place an image in the centre
   (b) place a word in the centre
   (c) place nothing in the centre
   (d) always place a word and an image in the centre
7 Using new super-speed and range reading techniques, you should be
   able to establish new normal speeds of well over:
   (a) 500 words per minute
   (b) 1000 words per minute
   (c) 10,000 words per minute
   (d) 100,000 words per minute
8 The two companies that formed intellectual commando units for
   studying books were:
   (a) IBM and Coca Cola
   (b) Digital and Nabisco

    (c) Nabisco and Microsoft
    (d) IBM and ICL

9 Mnemonic techniques were originally invented by:
    (a) the English
    (b) the Romans
    (c) the Greeks
    (d) Plato

10 After a one-hour learning period, there is:
    (a) a short rise in the recall of information
    (b) a levelling off in the recall of information
    (c) a short drop in the recall of information
    (d) rapid drop in the recall of information

11 Twenty-four hours after a learning period, the following amount of detail is often lost:
    (a) 60 per cent
    (b) 70 per cent
    (c) 80 per cent
    (d) 90 per cent

12 The number of brain cells in the brain is:
    (a) one million
    (b) one thousand million
    (c) one million million
    (d) one hundred million

13 The IBM Roadrunner computer is finally approaching the capacity of the brain in its overall ability to calculate.   *True/False*

14 Dr Marion Diamond confirmed that there is:
    (a) no evidence of brain cell loss with age in normal active and healthy brains
    (b) no evidence of brain cell loss with age in any brain
    (c) no evidence of brain cell loss with age in brains under 40 years old
    (d) evidence of slight brain cell loss with age in normal active and healthy brains

15 With adequate training, statistically significant and permanent improvements in intelligence can be made in people up to the age of:
    (a) 60
    (b) 70

(c) 80
(d) 90

Check your answers against those on page 215. Then divide your score by 15 and multiply by 100 to calculate your percentage comprehension.

Comprehension score: _____ 0 _____ out of 15

_____ per cent

Now enter your score in your progress graph and chart on pages 222–3.

How did you do?

Now that you have finished your first self-test, you will have a base level from which to springboard. To find out where you stand in relation to readers around the world, consult the table below, which gives you a range of reading speeds and comprehensions from 'poor' to 'one-in-a-thousand'. You can use this table to help you refine your goals as you progress through the book.

Reader	Speed (wpm)	Comprehension
Below average	10–100	30–50%
Average	200–240	50–70%
Functionally literate	400	70–80%
Top 1 in 100	800–1000	80+%
Top 1 in 1000	1000+	80+%

Another useful yardstick on reading speeds relates speeds dependent on an individual's educational level (see Figure 1.2).

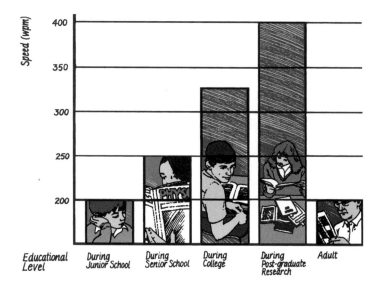

Figure 1.2 **Graph showing average reading rate throughout life**

The reason for the increase with education is due not so much to gaining knowledge of how to read better but to the simple pressure of having to read so much more material in such a compressed time.

In other words, *motivation is a crucial factor.*

Further evidence for this is provided by the fact that the adult, after leaving formal education, slips right back to the junior school level, primarily because motivation has declined and the pressure is off. The amount of reading is, on average, reduced to as little as one book per year.

Unlike the individuals surveyed, when you have absorbed the information in this book, you will not fall back to your previous low levels – instead, you will maintain and improve whatever level you have achieved.

Your reading speed now is: _____

Your comprehension now is: _____

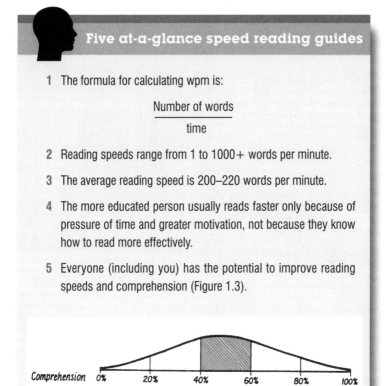

Five at-a-glance speed reading guides

1 The formula for calculating wpm is:

$$\frac{\text{Number of words}}{\text{time}}$$

2 Reading speeds range from 1 to 1000+ words per minute.

3 The average reading speed is 200–220 words per minute.

4 The more educated person usually reads faster only because of pressure of time and greater motivation, not because they know how to read more effectively.

5 Everyone (including you) has the potential to improve reading speeds and comprehension (Figure 1.3).

Comprehension   0%   20%   40%   60%   80%   100%

50% comprehension (most people)

Figure 1.3 **Comprehension curve showing comprehension rate for the general population**

Now that you have completed the introduction warm-up, the self-test and the comprehension tests in this chapter and flipped through all the pages of the book, let's learn how to control that ultimate digital camera and computer processor combined – your amazing eye.

Controlling your eye movements

In this chapter we discover some extraordinary facts about your eyes, investigate how your eyes really move when they read, and introduce you to five new ways to increase instantly your reading speed and comprehension.

Each of your eyes is the optimum optical instrument known to humankind. Each of your eyes contains 130 million light-receivers, and each light-receiver can take in at least five photons (bundles of light energy) per second. The nature of this miraculous instrument can be understood, and, being understood, can be controlled and used to your extraordinary advantage.

Variations in pupil size

We have known for some time that our pupils adjust their size according to light intensity and the nearness of the object. The brighter the light and the nearer the object, the smaller the pupil size.

Western scientists have discovered that pupil size also varies with emotion, and that if you are confronted with a sight that especially interests you, such as an attractive member of the opposite sex, your pupil size automatically increases. Such changes are small but can be noticed with careful observation. Jade dealers in China have been aware of this phenomenon for many years: when presenting objects for the customer's inspection, the dealer pays particularly close attention to the customer's eyes, waiting for an increase in pupil size. When this increase has been observed, the dealer knows that the customer is hooked and sets an appropriate price.

As a speed reader, if you are interested in something, your pupil dilates, letting more light in. In other words, the more interested you are, the wider your brain draws the curtains behind your eyes, allowing itself (and you) to receive, with *no extra effort*, more data per second.

Eyes at the back of your head

The phenomenally complex images decoded by your retinal light receivers are sent along the optic nerve and transmitted to the visual area of your brain – the occipital lobe. The occipital lobe is, paradoxically, situated not just behind the eyes but at the back of your head. No wonder we describe very observant people as having eyes at the back of their head!

It is the occipital lobe of the brain that actually does the reading, directing your eyes around the page to hunt for information that is of interest to your brain. This knowledge forms the basis of the revolutionary approach to speed reading that will unfold in the next few chapters.

Knowing these amazing new facts about the eyes, it becomes clear that traditional reading habits and reading speeds must be a product of mistraining and misuse; and that if our eyes were understood and trained properly their functions would significantly improve.

Reading involves 'eye-jumping'

How do your eyes really read? An extraordinary fact about how your eyes really move when they read is that they actually make small and fairly regular 'jumps' (Figure 2.1). These take the eye from fixation point to fixation point, usually a bit more than a word at a time. So the eye does not move smoothly over the page at all. Instead, it moves in small hops from left to right, right to left, or up and down, down and up, pausing for a moment to take in a word or two before moving on and repeating the process (Figure 2.2a).

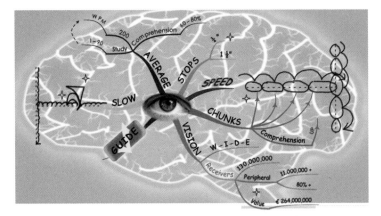

Figure 2.1 *How the eye reads. This Mind Map shows that the eye reads an average of 200 words per minute, with study (note-taking) speeds going from 1 to 90. Comprehension is on average 60–80% on relatively easy reading material – and that drops after 24 hours to a memory recall of 20%. So, if you are worrying about 100% comprehension, why worry about perfect comprehension? The fact is, you want 100% of* what you need *from that material, not 100% of* all *the material. That is a fundamental difference and, once you grasp this, you will lose that 'eye-dragging' fear of failure of comprehension. You'll always miss something so get rid of that worry.*

The eye actually reads in a start–stop motion, stopping to 'photograph' or to capture what it is seeing. The brain has to focus and the eye has to stop. Reading movement is not like a train on a smooth-running high-speed track but more like a chunking and shunting local rail service. It moves in chunks or 'fixations'; it back-tracks too. So, how do you read faster? By taking in more chunks at a time (rather than individual words).

We don't have to worry about comprehension because we already know that this is much lower than is assumed.

The other branches refer to the power of peripheral vision in helping us to speed read and what little percentage we use for our visual power. You might say: 'If it's in focus, it's either under control or too late.' One key to speed reading is therefore to 'uncouple' or disengage the brain from the clear focus and to re-read the whole page, 'hunting' with your wide vision. All these aspects of speed reading are explored in detail in this book.

Remember: your eye is an amazing instrument, with 130 million light-receivers taking in squadrons of photons – the data carriers – per second. Ultimately, speed reading is not just about books, it's about reading all facets of your life – social, personal, developmental – as you do when, for example, reading people's faces or reading nature.

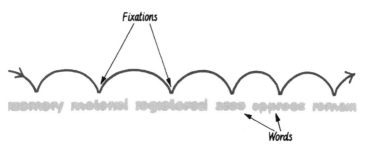

Figures

Words

Figure 2.2a **Diagram of the eye's basic progression while reading**

While the eye is moving and pausing, moving and pausing in this way, the information is absorbed *only during the pauses*. These pauses take up most of the time. And, as each pause may last between a quarter and one and a half seconds, it is possible to make an immediate improvement in your reading speed by spending less time on each pause.

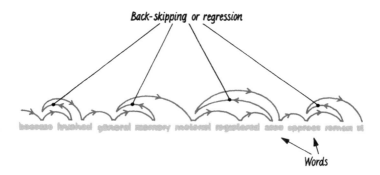

Back-skipping or regression

Words

Figure 2.2b **Diagram of a poor reader's eye movements**

Figure 2.2b shows the eye movements of a very poor reader. This reader makes about twice as many pauses or *fixations*, as they are commonly called, as are required for good comprehension. Extra pauses are caused because the slow reader often re-reads words, sometimes skipping back as many as three places to make sure that the correct meaning has been taken in. These habits of back-skipping (returning, almost as a habit, to words that have just been read) and regression (returning consciously to words that the reader feels have been missed or misunderstood) cause the poor reader's excessive number of fixations.

Research has shown that, in 80 per cent of cases, when readers were not allowed to back-skip or regress, they discovered that their eyes had actually taken in the information, and absorbed it, as they read the next few phrases.

The speed reader very rarely indulges in these unnecessary repetitions, which dramatically reduce the slow reader's speed. If each back-skip or regression takes roughly a second, and as few as two are made per line, then on an average page of 40 lines, *one minute and 20 seconds* are wasted. On a normal book of 300 pages, *one minute 20 seconds × 300 pages = 400 minutes =* $6\frac{2}{3}$ hours of extra wasted time spent reading (and not comprehending).

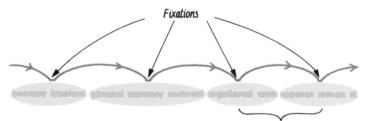

Figure 2.2c *Diagram of a good reader's eye movements*

Fixating without back-skipping

Figure 2.2c shows that the good or speed reader, while not back-skipping or regressing, also has longer jumps. The good reader also takes in not one word per fixation, but three, four or five.

If we assume for the moment that each fixation takes the same time, and set that time at an average of half a second per fixation, an interesting picture emerges: on a normal line of 12 words per line, the poor reader, fixating on one word per fixation and back-skipping or regressing twice, will take ½ + ½ + ½ + ½ + ½ + ½ + ½ + ½ + ½ + ½ + ½ + ½ + ½ + ½ = 7 seconds; whereas the speed reader, taking in three or four words per fixation with no back-skipping or regression, takes ½ + ½ + ½ + ½ = 2 seconds.

The speed reader, with a minor adjustment in the mechanics of the eye, has out-read and out-sped the slow reader by 350 per cent.

Comprehension: 'I don't get it'

'But wait,' you say. 'I have always been told that for good comprehension I must read 'slowly and carefully'. Surely increasing my speed will decrease my comprehension?'

This assumption sounds logical, and yet a little investigation shows it to be completely false. Research is increasingly showing that the faster you read, the better your comprehension.

To check this for yourself, read the following statement exactly as it is laid out, taking it in slowly and carefully and going for maximum comprehension:

> Speed read ing has be en found to be bet ter for under
> stand ing than slow read ing.

Difficult? Of course! Because your brain is not designed to read at such a disastrously slow pace. Reading slowly and carefully encourages your brain to read more and more slowly, with less and less comprehension and more and more agony.

Now look at the next sentence, this time reading the words as they are grouped:

> It has been discovered that   the human brain   with the help
> of its eyes   takes in information   far more easily   when
> the information   is conveniently grouped   in meaningful
> bundles.

Your brain works better at speed

Your brain works far more comfortably at speeds of 400 wpm and above. (It is interesting to note that, when most people estimate their reading speed, the speed at which they move their finger is in fact 400 wpm or more.) An increase in speed therefore leads automatically to an increase in comprehension. This is because the information is organised in meaningful chunks that make immediate sense to your brain. This increased ability to understand in turn helps you to remember better, because your memory is also based on your brain's ability to organise information in meaningful chunks.

Your first task, then, is to work at eliminating the unhelpful habits of

- back-skipping;

- regression;

- taking in too few words per fixation.

In addition to getting rid of these unhelpful habits, there is a fourth major way of increasing your speed. If your normal fixation time is one second per fixation, and you can increase your speed to half a second per fixation (which should be easy, remembering that your eye can take in information at one five-hundredth of a second), then you will have doubled your reading speed. Therefore, *increase your speed per fixation*.

EXERCISE

Visual gulp

The exercise that follows is designed to help you make quicker fixations and take in more information per 'visual gulp'. This should give you the confidence and increased motivation you need to eliminate back-skipping and regression. It will also encourage you to take in more at a glance as you read.

The exercise has been designed for people who favour either the left or the right hand. Use a card to cover up the numbers. Expose each number as briefly as possible, giving yourself no more than a split second to see it. Almost at the same time as it is uncovered it should be recovered.

Then write in the space next to the number what you think that number is, and check to see whether you were right or wrong. Continue to the next number, moving from column to column, repeating the process until the page has been completed. You will find that the exercise becomes more challenging as you progress, because the number of digits is gradually increased. If you can reach the end of the six-digit numbers with few mistakes, you will have done extremely well.

You will find that, with practice, you will be able to complete the six-digit numbers in one flash, and this will give you increased confidence to take in two or more words at a time as you read. The numbers that follow include just enough examples of each digit-grouping to allow your eye/brain to get accustomed to that level before moving you on to the next.

_____ 26 _____	_____ 53 _____
_____ 74 _____	_____ 79 _____
_____ 82 _____	_____ 63 _____
_____ 91 _____	_____ 73 _____
_____ 22 _____	_____ 53 _____
_____ 35 _____	_____ 29 _____
_____ 66 _____	_____ 24 _____
_____ 25 _____	_____ 31 _____
_____ 46 _____	_____ 02 _____
_____ 13 _____	_____ 85 _____
_____ 72 _____	_____ 43 _____
_____ 20 _____	_____ 67 _____
_____ 50 _____	_____ 76 _____
_____ 23 _____	_____ 06 _____
_____ 40 _____	_____ 28 _____
_____ 96 _____	_____ 88 _____
_____ 77 _____	_____ 84 _____
_____ 45 _____	_____ 15 _____
_____ 21 _____	_____ 60 _____
_____ 83 _____	_____ 49 _____
_____ 99 _____	_____ 78 _____
_____ 58 _____	_____ 87 _____
_____ 18 _____	_____ 03 _____
_____ 277 _____	_____ 864 _____
_____ 833 _____	_____ 825 _____

_____013_____	_____953_____
_____736_____	_____425_____
_____226_____	_____736_____
_____129_____	_____490_____
_____903_____	_____363_____
_____271_____	_____646_____
_____736_____	_____726_____
_____813_____	_____411_____
_____413_____	_____361_____
_____908_____	_____058_____
_____862_____	_____864_____
_____832_____	_____956_____
_____864_____	_____525_____
_____865_____	_____737_____
_____837_____	_____635_____
_____747_____	_____737_____
_____109_____	_____107_____
_____251_____	_____747_____
_____982_____	_____837_____
_____825_____	_____215_____
_____211_____	_____847_____
_____267_____	_____880_____
_____837_____	_____626_____
_____108_____	_____103_____
_____411_____	_____217_____
_____715_____	_____870_____
_____975_____	_____544_____
_____779_____	_____656_____
_____744_____	_____458_____
_____764_____	_____168_____

_____ 216 _____	_____ 562 _____
_____ 077 _____	_____ 541 _____
_____ 865 _____	_____ 655 _____
_____ 877 _____	_____ 668 _____
_____ 755 _____	_____ 302 _____
_____ 866 _____	_____ 110 _____
_____ 199 _____	_____ 617 _____
_____ 8638 _____	_____ 7475 _____
_____ 7875 _____	_____ 7356 _____
_____ 1178 _____	_____ 1088 _____
_____ 2277 _____	_____ 2436 _____
_____ 7426 _____	_____ 8656 _____
_____ 7655 _____	_____ 6423 _____
_____ 7777 _____	_____ 6555 _____
_____ 5433 _____	_____ 6545 _____
_____ 7657 _____	_____ 5433 _____
_____ 9880 _____	_____ 8702 _____
_____ 8612 _____	_____ 0188 _____
_____ 9871 _____	_____ 0677 _____
_____ 8766 _____	_____ 3343 _____
_____ 3777 _____	_____ 2244 _____
_____ 7544 _____	_____ 7702 _____
_____ 1074 _____	_____ 7653 _____
_____ 7654 _____	_____ 7623 _____
_____ 8764 _____	_____ 5433 _____
_____ 5325 _____	_____ 6543 _____
_____ 6423 _____	_____ 7056 _____
_____ 0653 _____	_____ 8765 _____
_____ 8644 _____	_____ 7655 _____
_____ 6118 _____	_____ 1154 _____
_____ 7703 _____	_____ 8674 _____

_____ 5423 _____	_____ 7534 _____
_____ 8762 _____	_____ 5734 _____
_____ 8277 _____	_____ 7374 _____
_____ 7272 _____	_____ 8862 _____
_____ 0177 _____	_____ 1761 _____
_____ 8767 _____	_____ 2345 _____
_____ 7654 _____	_____ 5433 _____
_____ 6511 _____	_____ 6531 _____
_____ 1075 _____	_____ 7120 _____
_____ 9841 _____	_____ 1106 _____
_____ 3753 _____	_____ 2754 _____
_____ 8297 _____	_____ 1173 _____
_____ 9275 _____	_____ 4828 _____
_____ 5702 _____	_____ 8567 _____
_____ 3089 _____	_____ 9861 _____
_____ 2850 _____	_____ 8422 _____
_____ 76542 _____	_____ 46533 _____
_____ 75252 _____	_____ 64322 _____
_____ 19866 _____	_____ 98011 _____
_____ 44904 _____	_____ 66255 _____
_____ 37621 _____	_____ 64533 _____
_____ 95412 _____	_____ 27549 _____
_____ 95339 _____	_____ 86422 _____
_____ 15155 _____	_____ 08436 _____
_____ 85369 _____	_____ 18643 _____
_____ 35438 _____	_____ 74323 _____
_____ 47721 _____	_____ 52741 _____
_____ 76208 _____	_____ 79285 _____
_____ 51915 _____	_____ 29477 _____
_____ 68224 _____	_____ 13655 _____
_____ 01678 _____	_____ 29371 _____

82102	35727
44627	64652
50664	45610
27392	82547
99266	21420
56439	47539
14733	49763
38657	95079
63644	91637
30080	26091
17533	14161
16843	08222
93867	49653
84611	42983
12548	60258
62938	46104
47250	51252
52952	83704
07650	15733
29332	62969
345783	987104
201896	916846
456782	376520
569832	238755
387513	452876
984764	045018
298436	112785
090769	234743
954137	564220
759484	887632
656892	876926

_____ 332558 _____	_____ 031410 _____
_____ 476831 _____	_____ 517195 _____
_____ 219575 _____	_____ 376490 _____
_____ 857393 _____	_____ 438753 _____
_____ 386280 _____	_____ 875316 _____
_____ 619474 _____	_____ 219564 _____
_____ 219575 _____	_____ 376982 _____
_____ 487615 _____	_____ 085377 _____
_____ 764973 _____	_____ 387520 _____
_____ 114874 _____	_____ 978564 _____
_____ 576330 _____	_____ 103866 _____
_____ 657894 _____	_____ 984372 _____
_____ 349715 _____	_____ 769103 _____
_____ 496511 _____	_____ 041673 _____
_____ 392588 _____	_____ 643192 _____
_____ 567682 _____	_____ 638726 _____
_____ 284191 _____	_____ 116794 _____
_____ 767936 _____	_____ 436795 _____
_____ 432615 _____	_____ 998665 _____
_____ 816155 _____	_____ 654732 _____
_____ 764130 _____	_____ 284938 _____
_____ 084503 _____	_____ 563982 _____
_____ 278402 _____	_____ 876944 _____
_____ 801019 _____	_____ 932548 _____
_____ 342988 _____	_____ 478902 _____
_____ 865014 _____	_____ 543790 _____
_____ 987655 _____	_____ 037686 _____
_____ 765839 _____	_____ 258765 _____
_____ 965411 _____	_____ 423699 _____
_____ 356794 _____	_____ 175894 _____

▶

_____ 763297 _____		_____ 538722 _____
_____ 090808 _____		_____ 443245 _____
_____ 578392 _____		_____ 121377 _____
_____ 578343 _____		_____ 987532 _____
_____ 013677 _____		_____ 467832 _____
_____ 284680 _____		_____ 538763 _____
_____ 998577 _____		_____ 105790 _____
_____ 334877 _____		_____ 857644 _____
_____ 876653 _____		_____ 664893 _____
_____ 189568 _____		_____ 356543 _____
_____ 987564 _____		_____ 467558 _____
_____ 958747 _____		_____ 465379 _____
_____ 836753 _____		_____ 556794 _____
_____ 001579 _____		_____ 567833 _____
_____ 378696 _____		_____ 189696 _____
_____ 276460 _____		_____ 354673 _____
_____ 287655 _____		_____ 801568 _____
_____ 765844 _____		_____ 968477 _____

Now move on to self-test 2. Apply all you have learnt in this chapter, eliminating back-skipping and regression, fixating for shorter periods of time, and taking in larger groups of words per fixation. Make sure you start your timer as you commence your reading and stop it the instant you have completed the reading.

The Plus One Rule

The Plus One Rule is simply the following: whenever you are consciously attempting to read faster, aim to read at least one word per minute faster than your previous highest speed. In this way you will not put unnecessary stress on yourself, and you will often find that you have increased by ten or more words per minute, thus comfortably beating your goal, which leads to increasing confidence and faster and more efficient reading.

During self-test 2, and in each of the subsequent self-tests, give yourself a Plus Ten Rule, in which your goal is to increase by ten words per minute.

SELF-TEST 2

Challenge your memory, by Simon Hemelryk

I've never had a great memory. I've forgotten birthdays. I've agreed to play cricket on the same evening that my wife and I are supposed to be having a romantic meal. And I rarely remember to charge my mobile phone, leaving me entirely unaccounted for during long weekends climbing treacherous Lakeland mountains while my wife pines at home.

I think I get it from my mum. She has spent her life forgetting where she put her car keys. She told me a few months ago that she was worried about turning 74 next birthday. She was only 72.

But for the sake of my spouse's nerves, if nothing else, I decided recently that I had to improve.

I was vaguely aware of bestselling memory-improvement guru Tony Buzan and as I Googled him to see what help his books might give me, I discovered that the UK Open Memory Championship – run by Buzan's World Memory Sports Council – was only three weeks away. Now here was a challenge. Could entering the competition and pitting my wits against the likes of reigning champion Ben Pridmore (who can memorise a pack of cards in 26 seconds) be the motivation I needed?

The championship's chief arbiter, Phil Chambers, was prepared to let me participate, but I needed a mentor. So he put me in touch with Ed Cooke, memory training author and number 18 in the Memory Sport world rankings.

As I sat at Ed's coffee mug-covered table in a gently dilapidated Brixton houseshare, the longhaired 27-year old took me through the basics.

'I'm going to teach you a technique which began with the Greeks and Romans, that will help you recall dozens of numbers, cards and dates in order – as you'll need to do in the competition – by converting them into images and stories,' he enthused in the tones of a youthful, but still eccentric, professor.

▶

We'd start with a pack of cards, he said. Memorising these would make up two of the ten championship rounds. First, I had to assign each suit a type of character. Hearts, logically, were family members, clubs, I thought, should be sportspeople, spades were professions and diamonds were musicians. Next, I had to give each number (and the jack, queen and king) a quality so that each card within a suit was distinct in my mind. So, for instance, cards numbered four were represented by thin people: the four of hearts was my younger sister, Lucy; the four of diamonds was Kylie Minogue. 'Now, you're going to learn a shuffled pack in order by placing each character along a familiar route, such as your commute,' said Ed. 'Humans are very good at remembering spaces. If you go into a room, the amount of information you take in in five seconds – the shape of the door, the type of window – is equivalent to a 100-digit number.'

I chose to place my characters around my maisonette. The first card up was the nine of clubs. Nine signified intelligence, I'd decided (as in nine out of ten in an exam), so Paul Sturrock, manager of my beloved Plymouth Argyle, was placed in the first card position: the bed. Next was Michael Jackson (the king of diamonds) who would be lying next to Sturrock. Freddie Flintoff was next, standing by the wardrobe, a lawyer friend, James, was in the hall and so on until all 52 cards were placed on a route that ran around the house, out into the street and down to the railway station.

After an hour's practice, I could remember almost the entire pack in order and even corrected Ed when he claimed that Viv Richards (seven of clubs) was outside Greggs the bakers, when he was actually in our downstairs toilet.

'That's lovely recall,' Ed said.

I'm brilliant – a new memory king!

But Ed had deflating news. 'For the championship, you need to think of characters for the numbers 40 to 100, so you can recall random two-digit numbers and dates. You'll also need ten to 15 routes, because some of your competitors will be able to recall hundreds of numbers in ten minutes. Then there's the names-and-faces round, the abstract images and the binary round'.

Ed chuckled. 'Learning how to do all in two weeks will be a challenge. You'll need to practise for a couple of hours a day.' He ignored my concerned expression. He'd spent the last few weeks memorising Milton's *Paradise Lost* and was already able to recount three hours' worth.

I buckled down, though I'd only managed to memorise 80 numbers and characters by the end of the first week – 20 behind schedule. My wife helped by calling out cards and numbers for me to identify while rolling around on her exercise ball. I was grateful, but she had a tendency to sing out 'Five of hearts' several times in a row because I'd chosen beauty to signify the five cards and the five of hearts was, naturally, her. Conversely, she studiously avoided the five of diamonds (Scarlett Johansson).

With five days to go until the contest, Ed revealed that I should be aiming to recall 120 numbers in five minutes. With three days to go, my personal best was 25 in 20 minutes. I'd learned my binary numbers, but for the other rounds I decided it was too late to learn Ed's suggested techniques. I'd rely on native wit. Oh, dear.

I arrived at the venue for the contest – London's Simpson's in the Strand – to find the room laid out like an upmarket exam hall, with two competitors facing each other at each table.

Tony Buzan, who has the charisma of an eminent bishop, got things under way. 'This is intrinsically bigger than the physical Olympics!' he declared to the competitors and guests.

The first round was random word recall and I managed to write down 21 from a list of 200 that had been put in front of us for five minutes. Opposite me, top female competitor Katie Kermode scribbled away at a rate roughly akin to Jack Nicholson's typing in *The Shining*. The 30-year-old translator, who speaks four languages, must have remembered at least 60 words.

I was pleasantly surprised with the next round, binary numbers, as I managed to recall 60, but the names and faces round defeated me. During recall, I attempted only to identify two people and one was an Arab man in a head-scarf, whom I'd convinced myself was called Paul Tompkins.

Round four was random numbers and Ed's training paid off – I memorised 56 digits in 15 minutes. Then, in a cards round, I managed 16 in ten minutes. Katie had almost run out of paper to write down everything she could remember, but I still felt pretty pleased with myself.

'You're not last,' Phil Chambers told me at the end of the first day. 'Some of the other competitors have overstretched themselves and lost marks, but you're quite solid.' I was, in fact, second to last. I was ecstatic.

Outside the hall, third-placed James Paterson, a bespectacled young Welshman in a rugby top, was fretting about his performance in the numbers round. 'I think I got 5, 7 instead of 6, 7,' he said. '2, 4, 4, 8, 5, 7, 6, 8?' asked Ben Pridmore, a 31-year-old unemployed accountant, drawing on some of the 819 digits he'd successfully recalled (a new world record). 'Thank goodness,' replied James.

I went into the second day full of confidence – but it quickly evaporated. First, I made several mistakes on a five-minute number recall round, scoring zero. Then there was a dismal abstract shapes round and a dates round in which I scored a princely two. Suddenly, I was in last place, ten points behind a lad called Conor Muldoon.

Never mind – the last round was a quick-fire card memorisation. That's the nearest I have to a speciality, I thought. Five minutes later, it was all over. Eleven cards remembered. Not bad, but I'd let the pressure of attempting to be merely mediocre, as opposed to definitely the worst, get to me. I read the scorecard nervously. 'Conor Muldoon – 19 cards.' Damn.

Tony Buzan consoled me. I'd not been far off the pace in a competition in which Ben Pridmore had broken three world records and risen to world number one. 'My expectations are always high, but it's gone better than expected. You're competing at a very high standard,' beamed Tony.

And it got better. At the prize giving, I was delighted to learn that my overall score of 573 – though somewhat eclipsed by Ben's 7798 – was enough to place me 369th in the world rankings.

'Public interest in the brain has increased hugely during the last few years,' Tony reckoned. 'There are brain training computer games and bestselling memory books. And while the first World Memory Championship in 1991 had only seven entrants, there are now thousands of memory sport participants in 25 countries.'

So if my standing in the sporting world has marginally improved, what about my everyday memory? Since the competition, I've yet to lose my car and I've managed to organise a trip to my father's house, two football matches and a visit from my nieces without any of them clashing.

Impressively, after much practice, I can memorise a pack of cards in ten minutes. I'd be a wow at dinner parties, if only I had time to leave the house. And, best of all, I've even taught my mum to memorise ten cards in two minutes. She still has no idea where her car keys are, but it's a start. '

You must remember this …

You don't have to develop a complicated code or spend hours practising to learn everyday facts. Here are a few easy tips:

If you want to remember:

- The year the Titanic sank (1912), repeat this sentence: 'The media were going mad over this "unsinkable, titanic, behemoth" and couldn't stop talking about it nineteen to the dozen!'
- Which way you tighten a nut, think: 'Righty tighty, lefty Lucy!'
- Which country has the world's longest coastline, say: 'So why is the drink called Canada Dry then?'
- The correct way to spell 'recommend', say: 'I recommend you C M & M in concert as he's absolutely superb!'
- That 25 degrees Celsius is 77 degrees Fahrenheit, just recall that the queen's silver (25th) jubilee was in 1977.
- That the dialling code for the UK is 0044, say: 'The UK does have its fair share of 4×4 gas guzzlers on the road!'.

STOP YOUR TIMER NOW!

Length of time: ___*w*___ min

Next, calculate your reading speed in words per minute (wpm) by dividing the number of words in the passage (in this case, 1762) by the time (in minutes) you took.

$$\text{Words per minute (wpm)} = \frac{\text{number of words}}{\text{time}}$$

When you have completed your calculation, enter the number in the wpm slot at the end of this paragraph and also enter it on your progress graph and chart on pages 222–3.

Words per minute: ___*176*___

Self-test 2: Comprehension

1 What does Simon's mum keep forgetting?
  (a) Where she put her mobile phone
  (b) Where she put her TV remote

(c) Where she put her keys

(d) Where she put her hearing aid

2 According to Simon, Ben Pridmore can memorise a pack of cards in:

(a) under 2 minutes

(b) 26 seconds

(c) 35 seconds

(d) 59 seconds

3 Simon's first memory technique began with the
ancient Greeks and Romans.   True/False

4 In Simon's card system, who was the king of diamonds?

(a) Frank Sinatra

(b) Michael Jackson

(c) Elvis Presley

(d) B.B. King

5 Simon's memory coach suggests the amount of information you take in
in five seconds using locations is equivalent to:

(a) 5 mobile phone numbers

(b) 50 digit numbers

(c) a 100-digit number

(d) a 20-item shopping list

6 Simon's memory coach is learning which book off pat?

(a) *Paradise Lost*

(b) *The Da Vinci Code*

(c) *Harry Potter and the Goblet of Fire*

(d) *Use Your Head*

7 The venue for the UK Open Memory Championship is:

(a) Rules Restaurant

(b) Simpson's on the Strand

(c) The Strand Palace Hotel

(d) Strand Theatre, Aldwych

8 On day 1, Simon came where in the competition?

(a) 3rd

(b) 21st

(c) 2nd to last

(d) last

9 Simon remembered only two names and faces in
   the competition.   *True/False*

10 How many digits did Ben Primore successfully recall?
   (a) 101
   (b) 499
   (c) 819
   (d) 909

11 This was a new world record.   *True/False*

12 Tony Buzan started the first World Memory
   Championship in:
   (a) 2001
   (b) 1991
   (c) 1981
   (d) 1987

13 What has Simon gone on to achieve?
   (a) Losing his car keys only once
   (b) Memorising a pack of cards in ten minutes
   (c) Helping his mum memorise a pack of cards in ten minutes
   (d) A world ranking of 359

14 To remember how to tighten a nut say 'Righten
   lighten, lefty hefty'.   *True/False*

Check your answers against those on page 215. Then divide your score by
14 and multiply by 100 to calculate your percentage comprehension.

Comprehension score: _____ out of 14

_____ per cent

Now enter your score on your progress graph and chart on pages 222–3.

Having completed the first major chapter on improving the
mechanics of your eyes, it is clear that huge increases can be made
in your reading speed. This is the first of four such chapters that will
enable you to make similarly dramatic improvements. Before moving
on, it is essential to create a reading environment that encourages
excellence and success. This is the subject of the next chapter.

Getting the speed reading conditions right

Now let's look at ways in which you can increase your reading speed and comprehension by creating the right *external* conditions, paying attention to factors such as posture and lighting. This chapter also discusses how to avoid *internal* interference caused by problems such as anxiety and stress. Improve both external and internal conditions and they will react with each other in leaps and bounds to create even more positive effects.

Creating the best external conditions

Placement and intensity of light

The best light to study under is daylight, so, where possible, your desk or reading platform should be placed near a window. If this is not possible, and at times of day when it is too dim, light should come over your shoulder opposite the hand with which you write, in order to avoid glare and shadow (Figure 3.1). Desk lamps can cause eye strain if they are not positioned properly. The light should be bright enough to illuminate the material being read adequately but should not be so bright as to form a great contrast with the rest of the room. In other words, it's not advisable to huddle up to a bright lamp that beams directly on to the book. In addition to the desk lamp, it is best to have balanced general illumination.

Figure 3.1 **Diagram showing the best posture and position of source of light for reading**

Availability of materials

So that your brain can 'settle in' comfortably, your study environment should have all the materials you need conveniently placed and easily accessible. Not only will this improve your concentration and comprehension, but also it will be a psychological boost. Knowing that your materials are pleasingly and functionally placed increases your enjoyment of the task at hand and makes it easier for you to perform it.

A chair for physical comfort and support

Ideally your chair should be neither too hard nor too soft, should have a straight back (a sloping one causes bad posture and back strain and makes proper note-taking uncomfortable), and in general should make you neither too relaxed nor too tense. The chair should support you and encourage good posture. Kneeling chairs are a useful option because they encourage a naturally enhanced posture. When you sit on a kneeling chair you can straighten up and balance the spine properly over the pelvis. You will need to get up from time to time to stretch your legs and encourage blood flow.

Avoid 'comfy' chairs. Many people look for the most comfortable and inviting easy-chair in the house, pad it even further with soft cushions, place a footrest in front of it so that they can stretch out more comfortably, prepare a hot drink, and then settle down to two hours of intensive work – only to find two hours later that they have been dozing throughout.

Height of chair and desk

The heights of your chair and your desk are important: the chair should be high enough to allow your thighs to be parallel with the floor or slightly raised from parallel. This will ensure that the main pressure for seating is taken by the main sitting bones at the base of the hips. Sometimes a small stool or telephone directory can help to raise your feet to a comfortable level. Look for a desk height of 73–81 cm (29–32 inches); on average, the desk should be approximately 20 cm (8 inches) above the seat of the chair. The height of your chair and desk, the distance of your eyes from the reading material, your physical comfort and your posture are all intimately interlinked.

Distance of your eyes from the reading material

The distance of your eyes from the reading material should be approximately 50 cm (20 inches), a natural distance if one sits as described above. Keeping the reading material this far away makes it much easier for the eyes to focus on groups of words (see the discussion of peripheral vision on page 79). It also considerably lessens eye strain and the possibility of headaches from reading. To prove this for yourself, try looking at your forefinger when it is almost touching your nose and then look at your whole hand when it is about 46 cm (18 inches) away from you. You will notice a real physical strain in the former and a considerable easing of that strain in the latter, even though you are taking in more.

Posture

Place both your feet flat on the floor. Your back should be upright and you should aim to *gently* straighten your posture. The slight curves in your back give you essential support. If you try to sit up so that your back is too straight, or try to flatten these curves, you will end up feeling exhausted.

If you are sitting on a chair or stool and are reading rather than writing, you may find it more comfortable to hold the book in your hands. Alternatively, if you do prefer to lean forward a few degrees over a desk or table, try resting the book on something so that it is at a slight angle. Above all, make sure that you are sitting on a firm base. Anything soft or too comfortable, such as a cushion that gives way, will ultimately send you to sleep.

Good posture means:

● **Good blood flow** – your brain receives the maximum flow of air and blood. When your upper spine and especially your neck are bent into a curve, both your windpipe and the main arteries and veins in your neck are constricted. When you sit up straight, the flow opens and your brain can operate at peak efficiency.

● **Good energy flow** – the flow of electrical energy up your spinal column will maximise the power of your brain. Adopting an upright stance while maintaining the slight natural curves in the spine has been proven to give the spinal column more power and springiness. Lower back pain and shoulder-aches are also reduced by upright posture.

● **Added alertness** – when your body is alert, your brain is alert. When your body is erect, your brain knows that something important is happening. When your body is bent forward or slumped over, it is telling your brain – through the inner ear and the balance mechanisms – that it is time for sleep, especially when your head is tilted too far from the vertical.

● **Eye coordination** – your eyes can make full use of both your central and peripheral vision. They should be at least 50 cm (20 inches) from the written material.

Environment

Your environment will affect your achievements. The place in which you read should be light, spacious, pleasing to the eye, well organised for reading purposes, decorated to your taste, and a place to which you would want to go even when you are not reading.

Because reading, learning and studying have for so long been associated with repetitive hard work, many people make their study area bare, dull and dimly lit, and furnish it with the poorest-quality desk and chair. Don't make your study environment into a prison cell; make it a space for light and calm.

If you doubt the importance of this, consider how you feel inside (internal environment) when a special friend greets you warmly and invites you into a delightfully prepared room (external environment). That is the feeling you need to create for, and in, yourself as you think about the place where you go to read or study. It should invite and welcome you.

Avoiding internal interference

Timing

This often makes the difference between completely understanding what you read and completely failing to understand it. Because of habits formed at school, many people have never tried to find the times of day at which they do their best reading or learning.

It is vital to experiment with reading at different times, for we all have different peaks and slumps in this regard. Some people find that they study best between five and nine in the morning. Others find they can study only at night, and others still that periods in the late morning or early afternoon are best. If you suspect that bad timing may be the cause of your inability to concentrate and comprehend, experiment as soon as possible.

Interruptions

Just as unknown words and difficult concepts break the flow of concentration and understanding, so do telephone calls, unnecessary breaks, loud noises, diversions such as email and mobile phone text alerts, radios and other items of fidgety interest that often litter your desk and air space.

Similarly, your own internal environment can distract you. If you are worrying about personal problems, or you are in some form of physical or mental discomfort or generally off-colour, concentration and comprehension can be significantly reduced. Note that if your posture is correct, your breathing will be deep and relaxed, which will, in turn, make you feel more relaxed.

The solution is to make your study environment sacrosanct and to arrange it so that it supports you. Little things such as putting your mobile phone on silent or diverting your phone to an automated answering service, having a humorous sign on the door requesting no interruptions, selecting appropriate music, and switching off your computer so you are not tempted to surf or check emails all help to ensure the optimum reading conditions. Also, try to make sure that your general life is more in order, and your reading, learning, understanding and memory will all improve.

Health problems

If you are going to undertake an extensive reading or studying programme, you should do everything possible to make sure that your physical resources are adequate to the task. Even minor illnesses such as colds and headaches will make a big difference to your intellectual performance. Never underestimate the mind–body–spirit connectivity. Regular stretching and eye exercises away from the desk, preferably on a short walk outdoors, for example, will give your sensors a break and make you feel better about yourself and the task in hand.

Having learnt how your eyes work, and found out how to improve the environment in which they work so that they can work even better, you are now ready to take the next major step forward: doubling what you have already accomplished by means of a revolutionary new reading technique.

Guiding the eyes

In this chapter, we discuss the eyes' need for a physical guide when reading and learn how best to use such a guide. We are talking about using a long thin object, such as a slim pen or pencil, a chopstick or a knitting needle. This chapter shows you how the guide works and how best to utilise it. Master this, and in one fell swoop you will reduce back-skipping and regression, improve speed and comprehension, and expand the number of words taken in per fixation. With such a guide you will find speed reading far more relaxing for your eyes.

Follow the finger?

When a young child is first learning to read, what is one of the first things he or she physically does? *The child places their finger on the page.* We immediately tell the child to take their finger off the page because we 'know' that this technique slows them down.

Why, though, does the child do it in the first place? The answer is to maintain focus and aid concentration.

Are we being logical, therefore, when we tell the child to remove their finger? For surely, if the finger were slowing the child down, the logical response, in order to enable them to maintain their focus and concentration, would be to ask them to speed the finger up.

This conundrum requires further investigation. Do you ever use a guide when reading? You'll be amazed to know that when respondents are asked this question, 90 per cent say they don't! Now answer the following questions:

Do you ever use your finger, your thumb, a pencil or pen or any other form of visual guide when you are:

- reading normally?

- looking for a word in a dictionary?

- looking up an item of information in an encyclopaedia or reference work?

- adding up a column of numbers?

- focusing on a point you are about to note?

- showing someone else a point on a page to which you wish them to pay attention?

- looking up a number in a telephone directory

Most people will answer 'yes' to at least half of these questions, and many 'yes' to all of them except the first one. The point is, virtually everybody does use a guide in different reading situations. The only place they don't is when reading books because they've been told *not* to – and the reason they've been told not to is because they have been trying *naturally* to do it that way.

Isn't it extraordinary that we all use guides when we are reading in virtually every situation, except normal reading, where we have been specifically instructed not to do that to which we are naturally inclined?

Indeed, the prejudice against finger-pointing is so deeply ingrained that, if you walked into a senior professional's office and saw them reading a book using their finger, you would immediately downgrade your opinion of their intelligence.

So, what is the truth of the matter? Is it better to read with a guide or without a guide?

With or without a guide

This two-part exercise is best done with a partner.

Part 1

1 In the first part of the exercise, you need to sit facing each other, approximately 60 cm (2 feet) apart, with your arms folded and your heads still.

2 Now one partner imagines a perfect circle about 46 cm (18 inches) in diameter. The imaginary circle should be about 30 cm (12 inches) in front of the eyes. The person who is imagining the circle follows its outline exactly with their eyes.

3 Both partners keep their arms folded, and the second partner looks very closely at the first partner to see exactly what the partner's eyes are doing. Do not exchange any information about what you have seen or experienced at this stage.

4 The partner who is imagining the circle should be feeling what it is like to move the eyes perfectly around its circumference.

5 Now reverse the roles, with the second partner imagining the circle and following it with their eyes, while the first partner watches their movement.

6 When you have completed the exercise, exchange information on what you both saw in your partner's eyes and what you felt while you were following the imaginary circle.

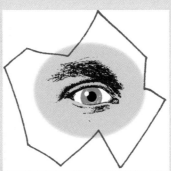

Almost without exception, this first exercise produces a shape that is very far removed from a circle. It is more like the battered line in Figure 4.1a, and most people find the exercise difficult.

Figure 4.1a **Pattern showing unaided eye movement attempting to move around the circumference of a circle**

Part 2

In the second part of the experiment, you and your partner sit exactly as you did for Part 1.

1 This time, one partner aids the other by tracing with their forefinger a perfect circle in the same place as the imaginary one was.

2 The partner who was not tracing the circle follows the tip of their partner's finger all around the circumference, noting how the eyes feel as they follow the fingertip.

3 The person who is guiding follows closely, as before, the eye movements of their partner.

4 During this exercise, do not whip your finger around too quickly or in multiple circles and do not try to hypnotise your partner!

5 When this has been completed, reverse roles and then discuss what you noticed about your partner's eyes and your own.

Most partners find that, in this exercise, the eyes follow the guide smoothly and are more comfortable doing so (Figure 4.1b). This is because the human eye is designed to follow movement, because it is movement in the environment that gives much survival information.
Once again it seems that the child was correct in their actions, and so were you whenever you used a guide to assist you in any form of information gathering. As this exercise demonstrates, eyes following a guide are much more relaxed and efficient.

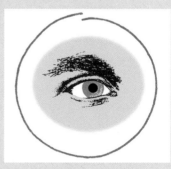

Figure 4.1b **Pattern showing aided eye movement around the circumference of a circle**

What's the best way to use a guide?

As your eye is designed to follow a guide, as you probably used a guide as a child for your normal reading, and as you have also probably used a guide in different aspects of your reading through-out your life, it is very easy to re-learn this skill.

As described at the beginning of this chapter, it is best to use a long thin object, such as a slim pen or pencil, a chopstick or a knit-ting needle. This way, the guide does not block your view of the page because you can easily see around it. For this reason, it is not a particularly good idea to use your hand or finger, unless no other guide is available, because the thickness of your finger and the volume of your palm will block much of your vision.

To make the most effective use of the guide, simply place it underneath the line you are reading and move the guide along smoothly as you read. Do not attempt to jerk it along in ideal fixa-tion groups – your reading brain will instruct your eyes where to stop as you move the guide smoothly along the line.

Moving the guide

An important question at this juncture is: do you need to move the guide along the entire line? The answer to this question may be found in the common knowledge that speed readers read 'down the middle' of the page. This is often misinterpreted as meaning that their eyes go in a straight line down the centre. This is not the case. What they do is to read down the middle *section* of the page.

This is because the eyes can see up to five or six words at a time, so they can easily fixate after the beginning and before the end of the line, thus taking in the information to the side (Figure 4.2).

The guide therefore minimises the amount of work your eyes

Figure 4.2 **Illustration showing the correct position for using the visual reading guide**

have to do, keeps your brain focused, and gives you constant accelerations in reading speed while maintaining high comprehension. It takes less than an hour to re-establish this mental habit.

In Self-test 3, you can combine what you previously learnt about your eye movements with what you have just learnt about guiding your eyes. It is advisable to practise using the guide for two minutes on material you have already read in this book and then to jump straight into the self-test.

SELF-TEST 3

Animal intelligence
Part 1: A Whale of a Communicator, by Mowgli

A Canadian scientist has found that killer whales speak a number of different languages in a number of different dialects. The differences between the dialects can be as small as those distinguishing regional dialects of any national language, or as large as those between the European and Asian languages.

Super-intelligent linguistic club

This finding places the whales in a super-intelligent linguistic club among mammals – a club that includes humans, major primates, and harbour seals. (Current research suggests that sounds produced by other mammals are determined genetically, although there is a growing band of researchers who consider that most animals are far more linguistically intelligent than we have previously assumed, and are species-wide and individually creative in their communication.)

John Ford, Curator of Marine Mammals at the Vancouver Public Aquarium in British Columbia, has been studying communications between killer whales for a decade. He observes that killer whale dialects are made up of the whistles and calls the animals use when communicating under water. These calls are quite distinct from the high-energy, sonar-like 'clicks' that the whales emit when navigating by echo-location.

Killer whales are actually members of the dolphin family, and are the largest in the family. Their name is a misnomer, there being no record that one has ever attacked a human – on the contrary there are a number of records that these whales, like dolphins, have often helped humans.

Whistling whales

Perhaps a movement should be started to have them renamed – the 'Whistler Whale' or 'Whistling Whales' would be more appropriate, apart from being more onomatopoeic.

Whistling Whales are found in all the major oceans of the world, from the warmest, in the tropics, to the coldest in the Arctic and Antarctic. The largest concentrations are found off the coast of the cool countries, including Iceland and Canada.

The population Ford studied numbered approximately 350 who live for the entire year off the coast of British Columbia and northern Washington State in America. The whales have formed two separate communities which roam through adjacent territories.

The northern community which consists of 16 family groups, or pods, ranges from mid-Vancouver Island to the south-eastern tip of Alaska. The members of the smaller southern community divide themselves into three pods and wander from the border of the northern community all the way south into Puget Sound and Gary's Harbour.

Fortunately, most sounds produced by Whistling Whales are within the range of human hearing. Ford's research is therefore easy to carry out – he simply dangles a hydrophone over the side of the boat, and amplifies the sounds electronically, recording them on a tape recorder.

Through his research Ford has been able to identify the dialect of each pod. He has found that, on average, a pod makes 12 discrete calls. Each member of the pod is able to, and does, produce the full set of whistles and calls. The system of these whistles and calls is different, both quantitatively and qualitatively, from those of other dolphins and whales.

Most calls are used only within a pod, but sometimes one or more are common between pods.

Common ancestors

Interestingly, Ford has found that these dialects are passed from generation to generation within each pod, leading him to speculate that groups which share calls are probably descended from a common ancestor or ancestors. The more calls two pods have in common, the closer the family relationship.

This phylo-genetic link between dialect and pod has enabled Ford to estimate how long it takes for a separate dialect to emerge. 'The rate of change appears

▶

to be very slow,' he says. 'It [a dialect] must require centuries to develop,' the implication being that some dialects could be thousands of years old.

One new focus of Ford's research has been the correlation between the behaviour of Whistling Whales and the calls they make. So far he has not found a great correlation, although he has found that calls are faster, high in pitch, and more frequent when an animal is excited.

Ford currently believes that, taken together, the calls form an elaborate code of pod identity which enables Whistler Whales to identify fellow members of their pod. This is especially important for keeping the family together when collections of pods, known as super-pods, swim together.

So far, Ford has not been able to identify a grammatical structure in Whistler Whale communication. But he is impressed by its acoustic sophistication: 'They seem to have a very highly developed, efficient way of communicating that is something we can only partly understand at this point,' he says. 'I think, as time goes on, we will get a much better appreciation of just how remarkably adapted whales are to their unique environment.'

Part 2: Dolphins, by Professor Michael Crawford and Mowgli

In terms of Rudyard Kipling's definition of learning as 'what, why, when, where, and who', many people feel that the cetaceans (the whale family) are 'three serving men short' because there is 'no evidence' that they can communicate on matters of when, how and why. Some years ago I was duty officer at Whipsnade Zoo when an unscheduled performance was executed by the dolphins.

One out of three bottle-nosed dolphins (*Tursiops truncatus*) appeared to be sickly and an attempt was made to catch her. The response was that her two colleagues closed in and swam in tight formation on either side of her, preventing the placing of the net.

The solution was to chase them into the small side pool and bring down the separating sluice-gate to make the business easier. The dolphins' response was one of great agitation, which subsided when they lined up again in formation and dived to the bottom of the pool. In unison, they squeezed their noses under the bottom of the sluice-gate, flicked it up and swam to freedom.

That rather suggests they were capable of dealing with 'how' and 'when' and, at the start, had certainly come to a conclusion about 'why'.

It is consequently somewhat senseless to try to compare the brain function of *Homo sapiens* with *Tursiops truncatus* without properly defining the ground rules. A comparison of function might be a more appropriate approach than 'intelligence'. Different species have different sets of problems and therefore there are different computer designs to deal with them. Some computers are very clever at handling ideas, whereas others are better at handling numbers.

This high degree of cerebellar development in the dolphin family is likely to be related to the fact that the animal operates in a three-dimensional manner. Like the birds, it has a requirement for coordination in three dimensions which the cerebellum serves.

In John Lily's famous work, blindfolded dolphins were found to be able to use their echo-location function to distinguish, at a distance, between objects according to their density. Such data suggests an interpretative system. Usually, the echo-location system is thought of as only offering a means whereby the dolphin can locate its food. A range of the dolphin's calibre, used for discrimination, has to be matched by a neuronal network capable of making sense out of the signal-to-noise ratios, just as we make sense out of what we see with our eyes.

A glance at a baby dolphin's brain suggests a dense rather than loose neuronal packing, and as each neurone makes 6000 or more connections with other neurones, the likelihood that such a brain does little or nothing with its sensory inputs is, I would suggest, rather remote.

It is possible, for example, that the capacity of the dolphin brain offers it a potential for memorising audio maps of the ocean geography. Indeed, as fisher folk know, the fish and squid are not just found anywhere but in their own feeding grounds which relate to the geography and geology of the ocean, its current, rock and other formations on which marine life grows.

The dolphin may, for all we know, 'see' sound. It is an extraordinary fact that some people who are unusually gifted with memory may actually talk of hearing colour and seeing sound.

This might be expected from an unusually large number of synaptic connections enabling the brain to cross-reference information to a higher degree. If that is conceivable, is it not also possible that our view of the cetaceans' inability to communicate, based on the poor variety of the noises they make, is misleading? Just because we communicate with words in the middle range of our audio detection frequency, does that mean the cetaceans have to do the same? With such a wide frequency range at their disposal, they may be doing absolutely nothing, or a lot, without knowing about it. If a dolphin did take a view on our capabilities in using sound, it would, I suspect, be that we are pretty primitive!

The trouble is that we analyse other species by relating them to ourselves. People often conclude that dogs and other animals are highly intelligent because they can perform simple tricks if we train them. The fact that *Homo sapiens* can capture cetaceans, place them in sensory-deprived environments and make them perform as basketball players to get their food, simply demonstrates the power of certain conditioning techniques, and perhaps the wasting of an opportunity to establish greater communication between the species.

Reducing the vast intelligence of these magnificent animals to mere party tricks is a minimalist, demeaning and ultimately unrewarding approach.

We would display our own intelligence and humanity more adequately by examining the vast range of abilities of our fellow creatures more humanely and intelligently.

STOP YOUR TIMER NOW!

Length of time: _____/ 0_____ min

Next, calculate your reading speed in words per minute (wpm) by dividing the number of words in the passage (in this case, 1580) by the time (in minutes) you took.

$$\text{Words per minute (wpm)} = \frac{\text{number of words}}{\text{time}}$$

When you have completed your calculation, enter the number in the wpm slot at the end of this paragraph and also enter it on your progress graph and chart on pages 222–3.

Words per minute: _____158_____

Self-test 3: Comprehension

1 Killer whales speak:
   (a) a number of different languages in a number of different dialects

(b) one language in many different dialects

(c) two different languages in a single dialect each

(d) the same language in a number of different dialects

2 Whales are in a different 'linguistic club' from that of
humans, major primates and harbour seals.   True/False

3 Killer whale dialects are made up of the whistles
and calls the animals use when:

(a) navigating by echo-location

(b) communicating under water

(c) making love

(d) warning of danger

4 Records show that killer whales have:

(a) occasionally attacked humans

(b) regularly attacked humans

(c) never attacked humans

(d) attacked but not killed humans

5 Whistling Whales are found in:

(a) only warm oceans

(b) only cool oceans

(c) only in the Atlantic and Arctic Oceans

(d) all the major oceans of the world

6 A family group of whales is called a nanopod.   True /False

7 Most sounds produced by Whistling Whales are:

(a) above the range of human hearing

(b) below the range of human hearing

(c) within the range of human hearing

(d) undetectable

8 An average family of whales makes how many discrete calls?

(a) 8

(b) 10

(c) 12

(d) 20

9 Whale dialects are:

(a) a false label

(b) passed from generation to generation

(c) different from generation to generation

(d) fundamentally all the same

10 Ford estimated that a dialect takes how long to develop?

(a) a year

(b) 10 years

(c) a generation

(d) centuries

11 John Ford, by studying the 'acoustic sophistication' of the Whistling Whale, has at last identified the basic grammatical structure in their communication. *True/False*

12 The high degree of cerebral development in the dolphin family is likely to be related to the fact that:

(a) it needs a large brain to communicate

(b) it operates in a three-dimensional manner

(c) its oceanic environment allows for greater brain size

(d) it has had many more centuries than human beings to evolve

13 In John Lily's famous book, blindfolded dolphins were found to be able to use their echo-location function to distinguish, at a distance, between objects according to their:

(a) shape

(b) texture

(c) density

(d) colour

14 A glance at a baby dolphin's brain suggests a loose neuronal packing. *True/False*

15 The dolphin's brain may:

(a) hear colours

(b) taste sound

(c) see sound

(d) taste colour

Check your answers against those on page 216. Then divide your score by 15 and multiply by 100 to calculate your percentage comprehension.

Now enter your score on your progress graph and chart on pages 222–3.

Immediately re-read this chapter quickly, using a guide to do so. Once you have done that, use a guide on the next newspaper or magazine that you read. Occasionally push yourself with the guide, reading a little bit too fast for comfort. This will gradually strengthen the 'muscle' of your speed and comprehension, in the same way that gradually using heavier weights in the gym increases your physical muscular strength.

You have now graduated from the lower echelons of normal fast readers to the first rungs of the speed readers' ladder. In the next chapter we break more boundaries by showing you the advanced uses of the guide and taking you into the realms of the super-speed reader.

Expanding your visual power

In Chapter 4 you discovered that your eye was capable of taking in more words per horizontal fixation. You are now going to do a series of exercises to prove that your perceptual abilities stretch far beyond even your current improved capability (Figure 5.1).

			hich you enter the /our central image, is d positions your central M
m	middle	image in the middle of	iy the same way as you d es and branches, each m in your computer. A'
a	b	c	d ^ch sub-branch

Figure 5.1 **Development of increased visual field in advanced readers.**
(a) Focus on a single letter, as when a child first learns to read by the phonic method. (b) Focus on a single word (the poor to average reader). (c) Focus on five words at a time (the good reader). (d) Focus on groups or bunches of words (the advanced reader).

EXERCISE

Measure your horizontal and vertical vision

*Figure 5.2 **Measuring your horizontal and vertical vision***

This is a two-part exercise:

1 First, looking straight into the distance and keeping your focus on a point as far away as possible, touch the tips of your two forefingers together, horizontally in front of you, 7.5 cm (3 inches) from the bridge of your nose.

2 Begin wriggling the tips of your forefingers and slowly pull them apart along a horizontal line, keeping your eyes focused in the distance (Figure 5.2a).

3 When you can no longer see the movement of the tips of your fingers out of the corners of your eyes, stop and measure the distance of your horizontal vision.

4 In the second part of the exercise, do exactly the same, but this time placing the tips of your fingers vertically (Figure 5.2b). Again, wriggle them and slowly pull your fingers apart until you can no longer see the movement out of the top and bottom of your field of vision.

5 Now stop and measure the distance of your vertical vision.

The results

Amazing, wasn't it? People often find that their horizontal vision is as far as their arms can stretch. The vertical vision is slightly less, but only because of the eyebrow bone.

How is this possible? The answer lies in the way the human eye is designed. Each of your eyes has 130 million light-receivers in its retina, which means that you have 260 million receivers of light in total.

What percentage of your eyes do you think is devoted to your clear or central focus, and what percentage is devoted to your side or peripheral focus? Fill in your answers below:

Central focus: _____

Side focus: _____

In fact, your clear focus has less than 20 per cent of the eye/brain system devoted to it, while your peripheral focus has a staggering 80 per cent. This means that, of the 260 million light-receivers you have working for you, over 208 million are devoted to your peripheral vision.

Why is such a large percentage devoted to this? The reason is that most of the events in the universe happen around your central focus, and it is essential for your survival that your brain be aware of every change in your environment in order to direct you towards what you need and away from danger.

In traditional methods of teaching reading, we have concentrated only on the clear focus vision, thus using less than 20 per cent of the visual capacity available to us, and using even that small percentage in an utterly inappropriate way.

Famous speed readers such as Antonio Magliabechi, John Stuart Mill and President Kennedy (see pages 84–7) all trained themselves to utilise the vast untapped potential of their peripheral vision. You can do the same.

Seeing with your mind's eye

You are about to perform an experiment in perception that will astonish you and will change you for life. What you will be doing in this experiment is disconnecting your brain from your clear focus and actively seeing with your mind's eye.

When you have read this paragraph, turn to page 83 and place your finger directly underneath the word 'memory' in the middle of the text. Keeping your eye totally focused on that central word:

1 See how many words you can see to either side of the central word without moving your eyes.

2 See how many words you can see clearly above and below the word you are pointing at.

3 See whether you can tell if there is a number at the top or bottom of the page and, if so, what it is.

4 See whether you can count the number of paragraphs on the page.

5 See whether you can count the number of paragraphs on the opposite page.

6 Can you see whether there is a diagram on either of the pages?

7 If you can see the diagram or illustration, can you clearly or roughly determine what it is?

Figure 5.3 **The Magic Eye illustration is composed of two pictures, each consisting of thousands of dots. It is your brain, not your eyes, that fantastically combines these into a clear image. This is the process that** The Speed Reading Book **teaches you how to use in order to become a super-speed reader. A clue to help you 'see' this image is that it relates perfectly to this book. (© 2009 Magic Eye Inc.)**

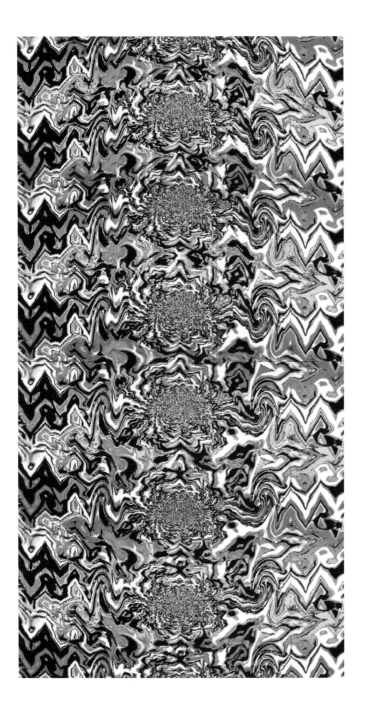

The results

Most people have no problems with this reading-with-your-brain exercise. This easy exercise demonstrates that your brain acts as a giant central eye that scans the entire world behind the lenses of your physical eyes.

Whereas most people spend their lives with their brains shackled to the tunnel vision of direct focus, the better readers, thinkers and survivors use the full range of their brain's visual skills.

Central eye perception

Your brain's ability to see with its central eye was well tested in the popular arena with the *Magic Eye* series of books. These books were based on the ground-breaking work of Professor Bela Julesz of the Sensory and Perceptual Process Department of Bell Telephone Laboratories.

Julesz's images are composed of two sets of finely woven dots. Each set forms part of an image. Each eye takes in a part, seeing only a flat representation. Your staggeringly sophisticated brain performs an astonishingly complex mathematical and geometric feat, combining both images to give dramatic three-dimensional pictures that are seen not in external reality but only by the brain (Figure 5.3).

Brain reading

The revolutionary new approach being offered to you in *The Speed Reading Book* is that, from now on, you will read with your *brain* as the central focus of your attention, and not your eyes.

Your eyes are a million-faceted puppet; your brain is the master puppeteer.

The super-speed reader of the future will be the person who combines peripheral vision with cyclopean perception (Figure 5.4) to take in, as the aforementioned Magliabechi was able to (see also p. 85), entire paragraphs and pages at a time – an accomplishment that, in the light of our new awareness, now seems far more attainable. One easy way to do this is to develop your fledgling skill with the guide into more advanced meta-guiding techniques (see Chapter 8).

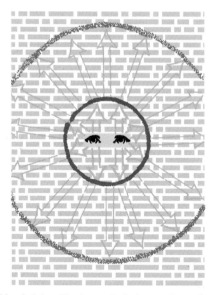

Figure 5.4 **Fields of vision. The inner circled area shows the area of clear vision available to the speed reader when the eye/brain system is used properly. The outer circle shows the peripheral vision also available.**

In addition to using meta-guiding techniques, you can also expand the use of your peripheral and central eye perception by holding the book at a greater distance from your eyes than normal. By doing so, you allow your peripheral vision to see the page far more clearly as you read.

The tremendous advantage of this is that, while your clear focus is reading the one, two or three lines on which you are concentrating, your 'brain reader' is using its peripheral vision to review what you have already read and preview the text to come. In this way, it is vastly improving your memory of the material you have already covered and is also preparing you for the material ahead, much as a reconnaissance scout prepares troops for safer and more speedy movement across unknown territory.

An added advantage of this 'soft focus' approach is that your eyes have to do far less tight muscular fixating. They therefore become far less tired and you feel able to go on reading for longer periods of time. Many people find that, by using this approach, stiff necks and headaches, a common problem for many readers, are eliminated.

Try using your brain's eye when you read anything. Continue practising with your guide, occasionally experimenting with taking two lines at a time. Always have your reading material as far away from your eyes as you can comfortably manage.

You have now made the leap from being a normal speed reader (focusing primarily on your eyes) to being a super-speed reader (focusing primarily on your brain).

In the next chapter you will be introduced to skimming and scanning techniques – fundamental methods by which we absorb *specific data* and glean a *general overview* of the information that we need to take in.

A quartet of famous speed readers

Here are four individuals who used speed reading to enable comprehension, concentration and retention of research and reference. This small selection of great political, scientific and philosophic thinkers indicates that speed reading, combined with the ability to understand, recall and use the material you read, plays a major role in achieving success.

Professor C. Lowell Lees

Professor Lees was chair of the Speech Department at the University of Utah in the 1950s. Without his knowing it, his reading speed inspired one of the major advances in this field.

A young student, Evelyn Wood, handed in her 80-page term paper to the professor, expecting him to read it at his leisure and return it to her later. To her surprise, he took the paper from her, completed it in under ten minutes, graded it and handed it back to her, as she sat in stunned amazement. Evelyn, who was later to become one of the leading figures in the Dynamic Reading movement, reported that Professor Lees really had read her paper. In the ensuing conversation, she found that not only was he completely familiar with everything she had written, including all her arguments, but also he was aware of all the flaws in her work.

Assuming there were between 200 and 250 words per page, Professor Lees had read and fully comprehended Evelyn's paper at a speed of approximately 2500 words per minute. Inspired by this, Evelyn researched the field thoroughly and later went on to teach reading at the University of Utah and establish her own Dynamic Reading Institute.

President John F. Kennedy

President John F. Kennedy is perhaps the most famous speed reader. This is because he emphasised his intelligence and mental capacity during his campaigns and made it publicly known that, having been a normal reader whose speed was approximately 284 words per minute, he had studied speed reading.

It became widely known that he worked at the skill until he had reached speeds of over 1000 words per minute. He also developed the ability to read at a great range of speeds, allowing him exceptional flexibility to vary his rate on the very different kinds of material he was obliged to read every day.

Antonio di Marco Magliabechi

Antonio di Marco Magliabechi was a contemporary of Spinoza, Sir Christopher Wren, Sir Isaac Newton and Leibniz. He was born on 29 October 1633 in Leonardo da Vinci's birthplace, Florence. His parents were so poor that they were unable to provide him with any formal education, and at a young age he was apprenticed to a local fruit dealer. Magliabechi spent his spare time in the shop trying to decipher what was on the pamphlets and journals that were used to wrap the groceries.

One of the shop's regular customers was a local bookseller who noted the young man's attempts to read the strange hieroglyphics before him. The bookseller took him to his own shop and Magliabechi was almost immediately able to recognise, remember and identify all the books. With the bookseller's help, Magliabechi eventually learnt to read properly and began to combine his new-found reading ability with phenomenal memorising techniques that enabled him to remember nearly everything he read in its entirety, including the punctuation.

A sceptical author decided to put the lad's growing reputation for speed reading and memory to the test and gave Magliabechi a new manuscript that he could never have seen before, telling him to read it for pleasure. Magliabechi duly read the manuscript at a remarkable speed and returned it almost immediately, confirming that he had read it in its entirety. A little while after the event, the author pretended that he had lost his manuscript and asked Magliabechi if he could help him to remember some of it. To his astonishment, the young man wrote out the entire book for him, transcribing perfectly every single word and every punctuation mark as if he had been copying from the original.

As time went on, Magliabechi read at greater and greater speeds and memorised increasingly large numbers of books. He eventually became so famous for the speed at which he devoured and absorbed knowledge that experts in all subjects came to him for instruction and source material in their own areas of interest. Whenever he was asked questions, he answered by quoting verbatim from the books he had read and automatically memorised.

His reputation spread, and he was eventually hired by the Grand Duke of Tuscany to act as his personal librarian. In order to be able to handle the volume of material in the entire library, Magliabechi decided to develop his speed reading abilities to an almost super-human extent. Contemporaries reported that he could simply 'dip' into a page, apparently absorbing the contents in their entirety with only one or two visual fixations, much to the amazement of those whom he allowed to watch him. He developed a reputation for having read and memorised the entire library.

Like most geniuses, Magliabechi continued to develop his abilities as he became older. The more he read and memorised, the faster he was able to read and the more he was able to remember. The story goes that, in his later years, he would lie in bed surrounded by volumes, each of which he would devour in less than half an hour, memorising them in turn until he fell asleep. This he continued to do until his death in 1714, at the age of 81.

If Magliabechi's eye/brain system was capable of such incredible reading and memory accomplishments, then why do the rest of us crawl along at speeds that make us functionally illiterate by comparison? The answer appears to lie not in any lack of basic ability but in the fact that we have actively and unwittingly trained ourselves to become slow. In other words, we have adopted belief systems, reading practices and habits that destroy our ability to read at any higher speed and with any reasonable comprehension.

Eugenia Alexeyenko

In his book *How to Pass Exams*, eight-time World Memory Champion and Grand Master of Memory Dominic O'Brien reports the incredible story of Eugenia whose accomplishments today seem to match those of Magliabechi 350 years ago.

According to a senior researcher at the Moscow Academy of Science, 'this amazing girl can read infinitely faster than her fingers can flick the pages – and if she didn't have to slow herself down by doing this, she would read at the rate of 416,250 words per minute'.

At the Kiev Brain Development Centre, a special test was set up for 18-year-old Eugenia, with a panel of scientists present. They were confident that the young girl had never read the test material before, because they had obtained copies of political and literary magazines that appeared on the news-stands that very day while Eugenia remained isolated in a room at the testing centre.

To make her task even more difficult, they obtained obscure and ancient books, and recently published books from Germany that had been translated into Russian, the only language Eugenia knows.

While Eugenia was kept isolated and entertained, the examiners read the test materials several times and took copious notes on their contents. They then placed two pages of the material before her to see how fast she could read it.

The result was as stunning to them as Dr Lees' had been to Evelyn Wood and as Antonio Magliabechi's had been to his contemporaries. Eugenia apparently read 1390 words in a fifth of a second – the time it takes to blink your eyes. Eugenia was also given several magazines, novels and reviews, which she also read effortlessly.

One of the examiners reported: 'We quizzed her in detail and often it was very technical information that a normal teenager would never have been able to understand. Yet she gave answers that proved that she understood perfectly.'

Remarkably, no one knew of the young girl's unique ability until she was 15 years old. At that time her father, Nikolai, gave her a copy of a long newspaper article. When she handed it back to him two seconds later, saying she found it interesting, he assumed she was joking. When he questioned her on the content, however, all her answers were correct.

Eugenia herself says: 'I don't know what my secret is. The pages go into my mind and I recall the "sense" rather than the exact text. There is some sort of analysis going on in my brain which I really can't explain. But I feel as if I have a whole library in my head!'

Speed Reading is like the

opening of a door into a

world thick with the **golden**

sunshine of knowledge.

HEINZ NORDEN, FELLOW OF THE INSTITUTE
OF LINGUISTS, AND FORMER INFORMATION
EDITOR OF *THE BOOK OF KNOWLEDGE*

Part 2

Focus on core speed reading techniques

In this part we help you 'up the pace' with easy and essential guided reading techniques that take in skimming and scanning, paragraph grasping and getting an optimum rhythm. We also highlight how the different meta-guiding techniques by your eye/brain system can super-absorb data from a page.

Super skimming and scanning

Scanning is a process in which you look for *particular informa-tion*. Skimming is a process in which you look for a *general overview*. Both of these skills are used by the vast majority of speed readers – and both can be enhanced by the use of guided reading. This chapter clearly defines the differ-ences between scanning and skimming and also includes some 'visual gulp' exercises to help boost your scanning faculties.

Scanning

In scanning, your eye glances over material in order to find a partic-ular piece of information for which your brain is searching. Scanning is a simpler process than skimming and is usually applied when you are looking up a word in a dictionary, a name or telephone number in a directory, or a particular piece of information in a book or report. The application of this technique is simple, as long as you make sure beforehand that you know the basic layout of the material you are scanning. This enables you to save the time that so many people spend hunting around in the wrong sections for the information they desire.

US President Theodore Roosevelt was one of the fastest and most voracious readers of the leaders of nations. He apparently started out with average reading speeds, which he decided to work at improving. His first steps included increasing his original fixation span to four words per stop, and then to six and eight words in a single fixation. Roosevelt subsequently practised reading two lines at a time and then began to zig-zag his way down the pages, reading small paragraphs with single eye movements. His approach was identical to that of today's leading speed readers. One of his favourite authors was Dickens, and yet the president still applied scanning techniques when reading his novels. As Roosevelt said in one of his letters to his son Kermit:

> *It always interests me about Dickens to think how almost all of it was mixed up with every kind of cheap, second-rate matter ... the wise thing to do is to simply skip the bosh and twaddle and vulgarity and untruth, and get the benefit out of the rest.*

Scanning is a natural skill. You do it every day of your life when you travel from point *a* to point *b*, scanning the environment for directions, food, people, objects of danger and objects of fascination. In reading, scanning is a skill that grows rapidly with practice. The 'visual gulp' exercises at the end of this chapter will help in that regard.

Skimming

Skimming is more complex than scanning and is similar to the previewing techniques that will be discussed in later chapters. Skimming can be defined as the process in which your eye covers certain preselected sections of the material in order to gain a general overview of that material.

The basic aim of skimming is to provide a fundamental architecture on which the bricks and mortar can be placed. An excellent metaphor for skimming was developed by Dr Nila Banton Smith, of the Reading Institute of New York University. Under the title *Swallows Skim – So Can You!* she says:

> *The swallow skims swiftly through the air, catching and devouring insects while simultaneously flapping his wings to propel his body. He even drinks as he skims along over*

brooks, ponds and rivers, gathering drops of water in his beak with no cessation in flight. This versatile creature doesn't pause or labour over any one insect or any one pool.

The swallow's mode of skimming for food and water may be likened to the method used by skilled readers who skim over pages of print, gathering what they want as they 'fly' along. With instruction on practice a reader can become extremely adept in 'catching' what he desires from reading while 'on the wing'. This is the type of reading in which some people reach 1000 words per minute and are able to repeat the gist of what they have read.'

EXERCISE

Visual gulp

Complete the scanning exercises that follow below.

1 There are six matrices. Each matrix contains columns and rows of numbers. The first number in each row is repeated somewhere across that row, and it is your task to spot it as quickly as possible.

2 Start timing yourself and, with a pencil in one hand, quickly check off the number in the row that corresponds to the number in the left-hand column.

3 When you have done all the rows on that page, record your time at the bottom.

Note:

● The exercises get more difficult as they progress, because the numbers get bigger and also more similar.

● By training in this way, you will be expanding the visual range of your mind's eye, which will help you develop both your skimming and scanning abilities.

● You may do these exercises in small bites or all at once if you wish. It is important when you do them that you are as mentally alert as possible, so make sure your eyes are fresh and that you are highly motivated.

Matrix 1

28	93	74	28	57	29	39	77
46	77	88	46	37	64	28	42
52	85	33	68	86	94	52	44
59	66	33	75	39	59	92	58
63	55	28	70	63	34	22	96
77	64	77	54	28	32	63	55
96	68	44	27	96	62	51	54
67	79	67	44	27	29	88	65
11	96	02	55	11	66	33	72
95	88	95	44	42	66	44	27
34	88	66	35	29	39	47	34
42	24	42	77	55	39	92	44
28	55	84	28	66	89	38	65
18	12	20	77	49	19	46	18
85	55	32	77	36	85	33	59
37	77	24	55	69	21	37	15
25	54	25	57	79	95	24	13
13	68	55	22	90	44	48	13
57	88	57	44	25	77	52	44
78	87	35	26	62	78	44	28
20	88	66	20	24	48	58	33
29	27	52	68	35	29	49	43

Time: _____

Matrix 2

675	568	675	875	639	891	569
625	874	271	018	625	735	906
672	672	875	236	438	282	239
911	743	343	554	277	911	902
764	543	674	764	246	665	322
879	772	544	754	272	879	647
753	258	266	372	753	348	236
844	766	343	568	844	236	543
877	565	235	877	655	235	568
822	544	822	654	266	388	419
103	202	547	103	654	813	113
457	790	235	252	457	746	322
238	198	674	368	238	636	638
848	765	638	848	636	426	853
847	784	737	636	782	844	847
336	772	327	874	336	764	873
379	673	838	379	737	892	811
282	537	282	987	254	654	272
444	765	238	444	266	782	754
658	690	343	562	676	658	824

Time: _____

Matrix 3

573	257	763	573	528	654	863
783	279	873	783	434	575	277
331	304	431	331	031	765	333
320	194	392	194	320	492	340
446	546	555	446	676	466	235
355	544	335	355	346	555	436
214	232	124	214	332	113	239
436	544	335	555	435	436	535
222	113	222	322	122	213	125
737	674	377	377	674	764	737
242	242	413	215	413	241	113
568	766	568	676	658	578	652
022	211	022	103	111	202	122
228	728	773	273	723	278	228
647	665	647	662	465	447	467
190	190	919	892	982	199	820
772	118	772	718	712	172	178
927	630	963	627	967	370	927
203	023	021	203	221	211	202
357	366	564	357	766	537	636

Time: _____

Matrix 4

120	992	192	117	911	200	120
554	336	354	554	332	552	355
013	121	103	022	013	105	212
483	485	483	249	429	825	843
217	613	622	262	217	127	617
528	726	276	528	753	258	573
2435	4427	6579	6755	2346	2435	2344
7877	7876	7868	7877	4568	3426	1988
3457	3457	7820	5433	7690	4564	2346
5683	3247	5622	5683	7622	8733	1957
1895	1949	1895	4527	7633	7683	1673
2215	2242	5623	6783	2212	2215	4125
5463	5463	8727	5673	7890	6533	0014
6782	1986	6722	6782	7629	9653	1935
5673	6582	8727	6739	6258	5268	5673
1873	1837	1873	8727	7628	1827	7828
2002	1003	0012	2002	1774	1021	1030
2680	8767	8687	6547	6438	2680	7444
7555	8665	5379	8677	7555	7677	5435
0865	0865	8766	7555	8776	5442	1645

Time: _____

Matrix 5

7524	6887	3568	4679	3479	5428	7524
8643	3569	8765	4589	8643	7544	3469
8532	6689	4489	8532	0166	1088	4672
8641	8651	6752	5572	7645	1754	8641
7302	1852	7411	7633	7302	0176	3467
3469	8533	4682	8752	3469	7632	8643
2458	7642	8644	4677	2458	8764	2476
7532	8642	3569	7644	1036	7532	8634
1876	1734	0568	8754	1876	8642	7433
8744	7533	7634	5689	8744	8754	3468
8756	8756	8876	5690	9756	4582	9752
8737	8762	8737	7755	7448	3569	7352
3469	7644	8876	3469	8754	1766	8442
1752	1751	1752	1742	8727	8764	8742
1978	1192	1978	7920	9772	8762	7792
8755	6755	8755	8548	8458	8745	8756
7654	7654	3368	3568	3568	5764	5369
1975	1975	1965	9148	7492	1948	1750
7865	7879	1756	7847	7865	4688	8747
8644	8649	8764	3487	8348	8644	3478

Time: _____

Matrix 6

8455	8456	8677	8455	4588	4585	8766
1176	1185	1766	1752	1158	1176	7642
8644	8638	8644	8642	4387	4369	8766
6433	2347	6434	6543	6433	3426	5433
8754	5785	8754	8763	4754	8736	3569
5242	8362	5413	7652	5242	8655	5243
7646	7655	7646	4766	5477	4578	5648
8412	8115	8412	1842	8712	4562	4812
8747	8765	4678	6489	7655	6875	8747
2575	2676	2676	2746	2575	4528	4453
7171	7702	7111	7172	7102	7171	0702
8742	7842	1875	8742	7815	1479	1785
4785	4789	4785	8748	8755	4785	4789
7633	7633	7624	2377	6738	2374	3729
3452	3435	3452	3542	1436	1544	5135
7634	7664	7337	7764	6734	7634	7637
8736	7854	6538	8736	8754	3579	9358

Time: _____

To further improve your scanning skills, spend ten minutes scanning a dictionary for words that you know and enjoy but cannot define precisely. Practise scanning and skimming skills on everything you read from now on. These skills you have just learnt are ideal for getting your brain into what athletes describe as 'the zone'. The next chapter shows you how you can preselect paragraphs to gain a general overview via scanning and skimming.

Power up your paragraphs

In the previous chapter we discussed the process of skimming, in which certain preselected sections of the material are covered in order to gain a general overview. In this chapter we shall discuss the structure of the paragraph, thus enabling you to further practise your skimming techniques.

Explanatory paragraphs

These are paragraphs in which the writer sets out to explain a certain concept or point of view. They will generally be quite easy to recognise and should be fairly easy to understand. The first sentence or two of an explanatory paragraph will give you a general idea of what is going to be explained or discussed, the last sentence or two will contain the result or conclusion, and the middle of the paragraph will contain the details. Depending on your goal in reading you will, in the initial skimming, be able to direct your attention appropriately.

Descriptive paragraphs

Descriptive paragraphs usually set the scene or expand on ideas that have been introduced previously. Such paragraphs usually embellish and therefore are often less important than those that introduce main elements. Of course there are exceptions, in which the description of people or objects is vital. In such cases, you will usually be aware of this importance and be able to focus your attention appropriately.

Linking paragraphs

These are paragraphs that join others together. As such, they often contain key information, because they tend to summarise the content of what has preceded and what follows. For example: 'The theory of evolution explained above will now be placed in the context of the latest developments in the field of biochemical genetic research.' In this brief sentence, we have been given an extraordinary amount of information, information that encapsulates the content of part of the material we are reading. Linking paragraphs, then, can be very useful as guides and as tools for previewing and reviewing.

The structure and position of paragraphs

How can you make use of the structure of paragraphs and their placing in the text in order to improve your reading efficiency? The most important point is to realise that in newspaper and magazine articles the first and last few paragraphs usually contain most of the significant information, whereas the middle paragraphs tend to contain the details. If the material you are reading is of this type, concentrate, when skimming, on the opening and closing paragraphs. (See also Chapter 15 for more on speed reading the media.)

Other writers 'clear their throats' at the beginning, before getting down to the meat of their presentation, which is then contained in the third or fourth paragraphs; in such cases, it is these paragraphs on which you should concentrate initially.

There are two games you can play with the structure of paragraphs that help enormously in understanding and maintaining involvement. The first of these is to make up, as you read, a 'memory word' for the main theme and the secondary theme of each paragraph. This exercise forces you to remain involved with the material and makes you think about it as you read it. Ultimately, you should aim at developing the ability to select these words as you read, without any pause or interruption to the flow of your reading. It is possible, by using these key words, to memorise the details of an entire book. Indeed, using key memory words in conjunction with images provides the basic building blocks of Mind Maps (see *The Mind Map Book*). Try this first paragraph game on at least four different paragraphs.

The second of the paragraph games is to relate, as you read through the paragraph, the first sentence to the remainder, asking yourself whether this sentence:

● is introductory;

● is transitional;

● is encompassing;

● has nothing to do with the words that follow it.

Do this second paragraph game on at least four different paragraphs.

Knowing how to analyse paragraphs has given you analytical power over the material you read. And you can continue increasing your reading speed in the next chapter, as I introduce nine different, interlinked, practical guided reading techniques.

Nine ways to guided speed reading

This chapter provides you with nine major practical guiding techniques to help you strengthen and gain control of your peripheral vision and your central eye perception.

Your photographic memory capacity

Open this book at any page and glance at the page for one second – can you remember any word, graph, shape or sentence? Would you recognise the page again? As we now know, we *do* take the information in. If you are in doubt, think of what your eyes immediately take in when you suddenly drive round a bend on a mountain road: many cars and lorries coming towards you, many going in the same direction as you; tens of thousands of trees, hundreds of houses and possibly birds and animals as well. All this is done in a fraction of a second. Think how tiny, by comparison, a mere few words on a page is – you *can* do it!

The skills you are about to learn will enable you to experiment with accelerated reading movements that take into account both your vertical and horizontal peripheral vision. You will be combining your peripheral vision, your central eye/focus, and the astonishingly quick photographic ability of your eye/brain system.

These techniques can be used for previewing; for skimming and scanning; for surveying; as exercises to increase your reading speed; as exercises to develop your peripheral vision; as a general work-out for your eyes; and, as the best speed readers are finding, for normal reading. At the end of this chapter you will be given several practical exercises and exciting methods for establishing these new reading techniques and for increasing your speed.

Guided reading technique 1: the double line sweep

The double line sweep (Figure 8.1a) is identical to the original technique you used for guiding your eyes (see page 66), the only difference being that you consistently take in two lines at a time.

To perform this exercise correctly:

1 Move your guide smoothly and gently along underneath two lines.

2 Lift the guide a fraction of a centimetre off the page on the return sweep.

3 Then move the guide again smoothly underneath the next two lines.

The double line sweep is an excellent way of getting your brain accustomed to using both its vertical and horizontal vision. This is much easier than you might expect, and many cultures use vertical vision as their primary vision; for example, Japanese and Chinese people have favoured vertical over horizontal for thousands of years. Similarly, musicians, as a matter of necessity, combine vertical with horizontal vision when reading music. If you can read music, you should be able to transfer the skill you have already acquired to double line sweep reading.

Guided reading technique 2: the variable sweep

The variable sweep (Figure 8.1b) is identical to the double line sweep, except that it allows you to take in as many lines as you feel you can at a time. Advanced speed readers usually take in between two and eight lines with each sweep.

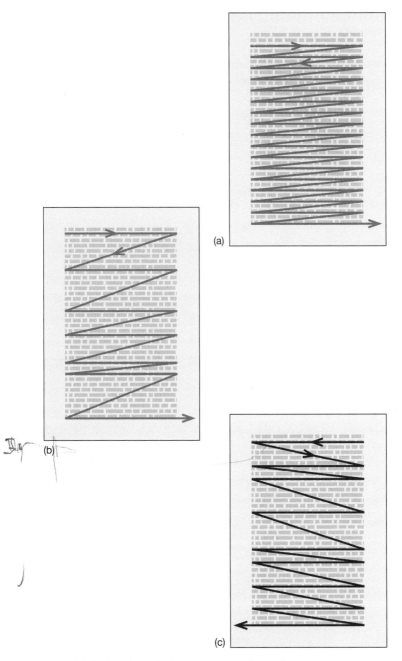

Figure 8.1 **Meta-guiding techniques: (a) the double line sweep; (b) the variable sweep; (c) the reverse sweep**

Guided reading technique 3: the reverse sweep

Simplistically this might be called 'backward' reading (Figure 8.1c). It has the advantage of allowing you to instantaneously double your reading speed by using the backward sweep of your eyes to take in information rather than simply get you back to the beginning of the next line.

At first sight this may sound absurd – surely reading backwards would simply leave a jumble of meaningless words in your head? – but it makes sense if you recall that your eye can take in information only by fixing attention and that words are viewed in groups of five or six. If you take in five or six words per fixation, which by now you should comfortably be doing, what you see in each fixation is in the correct order. Therefore, reading backwards is fundamentally the same as normal reading. The only additional work your brain has to do is to put large chunks of meaning in order, much like a jigsaw puzzle. Your brain always does this when reading anyway, as, for example, in the following sentence:

People who believe that normal reading speeds of above 1000 words per minute are possible are correct.

In this example your brain had to hold everything in waiting until it received the final piece of information, which made all the other words make sense. In backward reading the process is identical. Reading backwards is easier than you might think. After all, many cultures prefer reading from right to left, notably Arabic and Israeli. The reverse sweep uses exactly the same hand motions as the double line sweep and the variable sweep, simply reversing the technique.

The next six techniques are more advanced visual guiding movements. The 'S', the zig-zag, the loop, the vertical wave and the lazy 'S' can all be done at different speeds and at different angles. For in-depth reading, as much as 30 seconds per page may be required. For training, surveying, previewing and reviewing, ten seconds per page should be the maximum. The double margins technique, in which either a finger or a thumb goes down the left margin and your visual guide down the right-hand margin, is useful primarily for study reading and can be varied by making either the left or the right visual guide movement into a vertical wave.

Guided reading technique 4: the 'S'

The 'S' technique (Figure 8.2a) combines the forward and reverse sweeps. It can be used as a single line sweep, a double line sweep or a variable sweep.

Guided reading technique 5: the zig-zag

The zig-zag (Figure 8.2b) is a very advanced guided reading technique that makes particular use of the entire field of your peripheral vision. In this technique:

1 Gently move your guide diagonally down a few lines.

2 Then perform a little needle's-eye loop near the margin.

3 Sweep back diagonally down the page.

4 Perform another little loop in the opposite margin, and so on, until you reach the bottom of the page.

This technique, like the others, can be horizontally lengthened or shortened, allowing you to move the guide all the way to the margins if you feel the need, or to condense it into the middle two-thirds of the page, allowing your horizontal peripheral vision to take in the information near the margins.

Guided reading technique 6: the loop

The loop (Figure 8.2c) is similar in style to the zig-zag, the only difference being that the little needle's eye becomes a large area of text that can itself be taken in with one soft-focus fixation. The loop is an especially rhythmical technique and is a favourite among advanced speed readers.

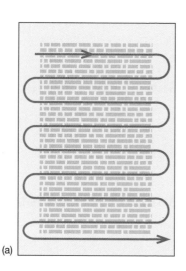

(a)

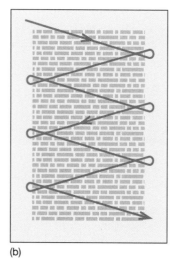

(b)

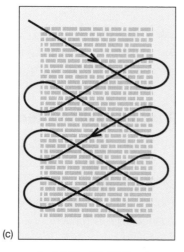

(c)

Figure 8.2 **Advanced visual guiding movements: (a) The 'S'; (b) the zig-zag;
(c) the loop;**

The Speed Reading Book

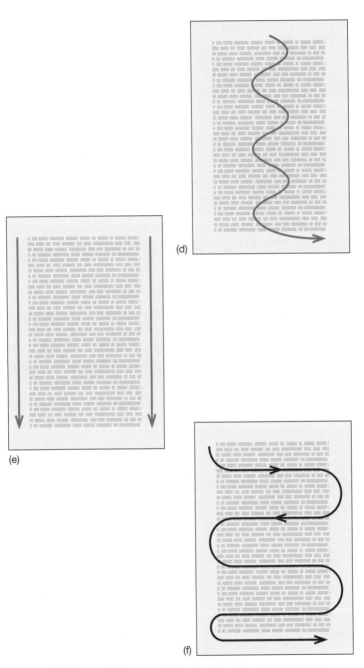

Figure 8.2 (d) the vertical wave; (e) the double guide; (f) the lazy 'S'.

Guided reading technique 7: the vertical wave

The vertical wave (Figure 8.2d) is the technique that often leads the uninformed to believe that speed readers read 'down the middle of the page' in a straight line. In fact, speed readers' eyes glide in rhythmical waves, moving slightly left and right, down the centre section of the page. The vertical wave is an ideal technique from this point of view because it combines forward and backward reading, also allowing your horizontal peripheral vision and the vertical peripheral vision to be used to their maximum extent.

Guided reading technique 8: the double guide

The double guide or double margin technique (Figure 8.2e) involves using two guides, often a finger or thumb on one side, and your standard guide on the other, moving each in unison smoothly down the page margins, while your eyes devour the information in between.

This technique is excellent for allowing your brain to dictate where your eyes go. If you have already established your general goals for the reading, your central eye/focus will search out the information. There is no need for you to force your eyes to fixate in particular areas. Your brain will take care of you.

Guided reading technique 9: the lazy 'S'

The lazy 'S' (Figure 8.2f) combines elements of the basic 'S', the zig-zag and the vertical wave. In fact, it could be considered to be a larger version of each. In this technique, you sculpt a large series of normal and reverse 'S's down the page, usually completing a page with five horizontal or slightly vertical movements.

Speed reader story

One of the most dramatic stories involving the use of guided reading concerns a 35-year-old woman who was attending one of my speed reading courses. The course consisted of eight three-hour lessons, each spaced a week apart. During the lesson when the guided reading techniques were being introduced, the class had to use the loop or the vertical wave or the lazy 'S' as a super-fast previewing technique on a novel. The time limit for completing the entire book was five minutes. The woman in question left the class in frustration, saying that, although she had used the guide on every page, not a single thing had gone in and she 'couldn't see the point'.

During the following week's lesson, the same novel was used for an exercise in which the students had to use any guiding technique and to read for good comprehension. The woman chose the basic 'S', and began, with the rest of the class, the 15-minute exercise. After five minutes the concentrated silence was broken by a shriek! The woman was screaming, 'I know it! I know it! I know it!' She reported that, as she became accustomed to the guide, the book suddenly opened itself to her like a film that she had already seen once and was seeing for the second time. What had happened was that her brain had photographed the entire book, storing it somewhere deep in her visual cortex and mind's eye. When her brain was stimulated again, it simply re-assessed the information and gave it to her.

EXERCISE

Visual gulp

The number exercises that follow will help develop your awareness of your vertical and horizontal vision. For this reason, each number group is on two lines. Uncover each block of two numbers and then cover them again, giving yourself enough time for only a short glance. Write what you think you saw on the line and check. When you have practised a few of these exercises, move on to Self-test 4. Before reading, select your favourite meta-guiding technique, raise your motivational levels, and go for your own personal speed reading record to date.

28	84
92	21 ....
94	14
07	68 ....
93	35

12	56 ....
86	48
74	99 ....
06	18
93	10 ....
57	39
72	51 ....
30	74
66	33 ....
73	84
16	28 ....
03	98
48	32 ....
71	39
95	18 ....
39	47
68	13 ....
96	70
04	15 ....
53	94
18	75 ....
08	29
42	65 ....
41	78
40	70 ....
39	73
15	31 ....
83	14
40	77 ....
56	93
14	36 ....
94	18

016	....	936	....
18		93	
964	....	148	....
68		25	
922	....	096	....
46		84	
921	....	695	....
04		98	
962	....	277	....
49		77	
763	....	194	....
91		04	
217	....	185	....
86		27	
103	....	976	....
93		60	
184	....	414	....
37		22	
629	....	050	....
94		32	
060	....	281	....
46		18	
299	....	504	....
37		95	
276	....	706	....
07		20	
330	....	063	....
13		30	
966	....	411	....
95		84	
563	....	392	....
52		78	

▶

380	153 ....
50	72
064	927 ....
11	63
693	832 ....
695	592
802	033 ....
938	153
805	408 ....
463	916
592	863 ....
907	106
818	763 ....
953	909
832	753 ....
711	063
393	494 ....
512	508
937	342 ....
830	174
148	673 ....
602	725
935	163 ....
291	408
175	853 ....
784	591
421	744 ....
594	422
208	906 ....
440	807
618	945 ....
128	705

483	912 ....
058	614
983	937 ....
163	731
975	147 ....
805	853
194	902 ....
254	395
110	707 ....

You are now ready for Self-test 4. While you are reading this self-test, make sure you take in large groups of words with each 'visual gulp', use your guide to assist you, and hold the book a good distance away from you, thus enabling you to make use of your peripheral vision and your brain reading capabilities.

SELF-TEST 4

Are we alone in the universe? Extra-terrestrial intelligences, by Tony Buzan

On precisely the day, hour and minute of the five hundredth anniversary of Columbus' discovery of America, the human race launched history's greatest-ever effort to discover not only new worlds but, more importantly, new intelligences.

On 12 October 1992, at 3pm Atlantic Standard Time, astronomers in Arecibo, Puerto Rico, turned on the most powerful radio telescope ever built. At precisely the same moment, others fired up a second telescope at the Goldstone Tracking Station near Barstow, California. More than a hundred physicists, astronomers, computer programmers and technicians are now assiduously monitoring control panels in eager anticipation as super-computers listen to millions of radio channels, searching for any signal that bears the stamp of intelligent life, and which confirms what the majority of astronomers have believed for years – that we are not alone in the universe.

▶

The 100-million-dollar project, called SETI (Search for Extra-Terrestrial Intelligence), has full NASA mission status, and will continue until at least the year 2000, in the hope of discovering radio waves created by intelligent beings: radio waves that might have begun their journey towards Earth at the speed of light as recently as yesterday or perhaps as distantly as ten billion years ago.

The mission dwarfs our previous greatest attempt at searching for extra-terrestrial intelligence inspired by the astronomer Frank Drake in 1974. Drake used the Arecibo radio telescope, which at the time had an effective power of 20 trillion watts, to send a coded message towards the great cluster of stars in the constellation Hercules, some 24,000 light years away.

The message, a kind of cosmic IQ test, was shown first by Drake to the astronomer Carl Sagan, one of the finalists in the annual Brain of the Year award, over lunch at the Cornell Faculty Club. According to Drake, Sagan worked out most of it fairly quickly.

The message, from top to bottom, shows:

1 A binary counting system
2 Molecules essential for life on Earth
3 Chemical formulae for DNA, our genetic material
4 A graphic representation of the double helix shape of the DNA molecule ending at the head of a human figure
5 A representation of our sun and nine planets (Earth is raised to show where we live), and a depiction of a radio telescope beaming the message.

The current mission is so enormous in its scale and precise in its engineering that we will be able to hear more in three days than we have heard in the 22 years since Drake began his initial experiments in 1970. In the new effort, at least six radio telescopes worldwide will eventually go on constant alert; the dish at Arecibo – 0.3 km (1/5 mile) in diameter – has been upgraded to increase its sensitivity by 300 per cent and extraordinary software has been designed to interpret signals. Drake, 62, is Professor of Astronomy at the University of California, Santa Cruz, and is also President of the SETI Institute in Mountain View, California. He says, 'I find nothing more tantalising than the thought that radio messages from alien civilisations in space are passing through our offices and homes right now, like a whisper we can't quite hear.'

The eyes

The largest radio telescope in the world is very different from the traditional optical telescopes used by amateur astronomers, or even the huge tubular telescopes that peer out of observatory domes and mountains around the world, like Palomar, California, or Mauna Kea in Hawaii. The Arecibo telescope is a 304 m (1000 foot) wide bowl of perforated aluminium set in a vast hole in the ground. Above the bowl, hundreds of tonnes of steerable antennae hang from cables that are connected to support towers on the surrounding hills.

Similar in design to a TV satellite dish, a radio telescope can focus every radio wave that hits it towards a central collection point where the signal is then fed to, and processed by, a receiver.

These 'eyes of the Earth' are so sensitive that, in 1987, a new super-computer connected to the Goldstone radio telescope in the Mojave Desert easily detected the faint, 1-watt signal emanating from the Pioneer 10 probe that was launched from Earth in the winter of 1972. At the time it was detected, Pioneer was billions of kilometres out in space!

Radio telescopes are especially useful in the search for extraterrestrial intelligence, because radio waves given off by stars are both irregular and random, while radio waves used for intelligent communication form patterns that are easily detected on display monitors such as oscilloscopes.

The idea of searching for non-random waves that would suggest the presence of intelligence originally formed in the mid-1950s in the minds of Drake and of physicists Giuseppe Cocconi and Philip Morrison at Cornell. In 1959, in the science journal *Nature*, Cocconi and Morrison wrote: '... the probability of success is difficult to estimate, but if we never search, the chance of success is zero.'

History's biggest bargain

To those who question whether the effort is worthwhile, Drake points out that the £135 million earmarked for SETI is less than one-tenth of 1 per cent of NASA's annual budget of £15 billion. 'When you factor in the consequences of success,' Drake says, 'this could be the biggest bargain in history.'

A large percentage of the budget goes on new computer equipment which both enhances the quality of reception and helps in the interpretation of signals.

These giant electronic brains will 'perceive' vast quantities of cosmic radio information which will be spread over millions of channels, and will sift through the data, culling patterns and possibilities for the human observers.

The brain behind these brains is extraordinary in its own right: physicist Kent Cullers has been blind since birth, and has never seen a radio signal on an oscilloscope, let alone a star. His passion for the universe stems from his father who, when Cullers was five, read to him from *The Golden Book of Astronomy*. 'The idea that there might be other worlds to discover fired my imagination,' he recalls. And his massive imagination is what is helping to give the Earth sight: he has managed to endow his automated signal processing programme with what *Life* magazine describes as 'second sight' – a system that can identify suspiciously intelligent signals in what would otherwise appear to be nothing more than a sound-cauldron of hissing static.

The head of the NASA project, Professor Jill Tarter, believes (as do her colleagues) that other intelligent life does exist. She and her colleagues envisage a galactic community of intelligent civilisations, too far apart to socialise, colonise or cannibalise one another. A message from any one of them, sent to Earth perhaps many millions of years ago when our civilisation was not yet existent, could reach us at any time. And what if the project does 'unEarth' the signals for which they search? Tarter says: 'Any signals that arrive are rightly the property of humankind. They were sent to the planet Earth, not to NASA. After millennia of wondering, all humans should know – we are not alone.'

Human as guardian

Arthur C. Clarke, famed science fiction author of *2001 – A Space Odyssey* and futurist, believed the search had tremendous scientific and moral value. In *Life* he wrote:

> However it might occur, the detection of intelligent life beyond the Earth would change forever our outlook on the universe. At the very least, it would prove that intelligence does have some survival value, despite what we see on the evening news.

SETI represents the highest possible form of exploration, and when we cease to explore, we will cease to be human.

But suppose the whole argument for SETI is flawed, and intelligent life has arisen only on Earth. It would, of course, be impossible to prove that – there might always be ETs just a few light years beyond our range of investigation.

If, however, after centuries of listening and looking, we have found no sign of extra-terrestrial intelligence, we would be justified in assuming that we are.

And that is the most awesome possibility of all. We are only now beginning to appreciate our duty towards the planet Earth: if we are indeed the sole heirs to the galaxy, we must also be its future guardians.

After millions of years of living in isolation, human intelligence may be within a mere ten years of realising that it has companions in the cosmos.

STOP YOUR TIMER NOW!

Length of time: _____ mins

Next, calculate your reading speed in words per minute (wpm) by dividing the number of words in the passage (in this case, 1406) by the time (in minutes) you took.

$$\text{Words per minute (wpm)} = \frac{\text{number of words}}{\text{time}}$$

When you have completed your calculation, enter the number in the words per minute (wpm) slot at the end of this paragraph, and also enter it on your progress graph and chart on pages 222–3.

Words per minute: _____ 175

Self-test 4: Comprehension

1   When did the human race launch history's greatest-ever effort to discover new intelligences?
    (a)   The hundredth anniversary of Columbus' discovery of America
    (b)   The fiftieth anniversary of the launch of the first satellite
    (c)   The five hundredth anniversary of Columbus' discovery of America
    (d)   On no particular historical day

2   SETI stands for Searching for Extra-Territorial Intellects.   *True*/False

3 NASA is searching for radio waves that might have begun their journey
   towards Earth at the speed of light as distantly as:
   (a) a million years ago
   (b) a hundred million years ago
   (c) a billion years ago
   (d) ten billion years ago

4 The previous greatest attempt at searching for extra-terrestrial beings in
   1974 was inspired by:
   (a) Frank Drake
   (b) Carl Sagan
   (c) President Kennedy
   (d) Mensa

5 The 1974 attempt sent a coded message towards the great cluster of
   stars in the constellation known as:
   (a) Jupiter
   (b) Orion
   (c) Hercules
   (d) Scorpio

6 In that coded message was included a representation
   of our sun and nine planets.   True/False

7 In the new effort, at least how many radio telescopes worldwide will
   eventually be on constant alert?
   (a) Two
   (b) Four
   (c) Six
   (d) Eight

8 The Arecibo telescope is a wide bowl of perforated aluminium
   set in a vast hole in the ground. How wide is it?
   (a) 304 m (100 feet)
   (b) 152 m (500 feet)
   (c) 228 m (750 feet)
   (d) 304 m (1000 feet)

9   A radio telescope can focus towards a central collection point:
    (a)   25 per cent of the radio waves that hit it
    (b)   50 per cent of the radio waves that hit it
    (c)   75 per cent of the radio waves that hit it
    (d)   all the radio waves that hit it

10 Radio waves given off by stars are:
    (a)   irregular and random
    (b)   irregular and not random
    (c)   not random and irregular
    (d)   not irregular and not random

11 The brain behind the brains of the SETI search is extraordinary because:
    (a)   he has the highest IQ in the world
    (b)   he was originally not interested in astronomy
    (c)   he has been blind since birth
    (d)   he was originally a doctor of medicine

12 Who has been described as giving the Earth sight?
    (a)   Frank Drake
    (b)   Kent Cullers
    (c)   Jill Tarter
    (d)   Galileo

13 Professor Jill Tarter hopes but does not believe that
    other intelligent life does exist.   *True*/False

14 Arthur C. Clarke said, 'SETI represents the highest possible form of
    exploration, and when we cease to explore, we will cease to be
    _____'

Check your answers against those on page 216. Then divide your score by
14 and multiply by 100 to calculate your percentage comprehension.

Comprehension score: _____ out of 14
                     _____ per cent

Now enter your score on your progress graph and chart on pages 222–3.

Tips for practising the guided reading techniques

- It is especially useful to practise all of them initially at very high speeds, aiming for virtually no comprehension, and then to practise them immediately at your new normal speeds. In this way, your brain will become accustomed to high speeds.

- It is often best to begin by using these techniques on material that you have already read, thus accomplishing two tasks at once: reviewing what you have read and warming up your eye/brain system for the task ahead.

- When you have completed this chapter, practise all the guided reading techniques on everything you have read so far in this book. As you do so, try to practise at speeds that push you to the limit.

- Practise with each of the guided reading techniques for at least five minutes, varying your speed and depth of comprehension as you go. The five minutes is necessary to allow your brain time to get used to the technique.

- Practise guided reading techniques at wildly varying speeds. Many people find, to their amazement, that at lower speeds their comprehension is almost absent but at certain specific rhythms their comprehension suddenly becomes amazingly clear.

The guided reading techniques you have learnt in this chapter will be of particular help in acquiring the rhythmical reading skills you are about to learn in Chapter 9.

Accelerating your reading rhythm

In this chapter we explore the idea of tapping into your mental metronome. A metronome is a device best known in music used to mark time by means of regularly recurring ticks or flashes at regularly repeated and adjustable intervals. US President Thomas Jefferson, a famed intellect, described his reading speed as *'always calm, even stately, like the tick of a tall mahogany clock'*. Jefferson had intuitively recognised and foreseen the development of rhythmical reading and the metronome method. With fine tuning, your eye/brain system can adjust to faster relative rhythms or beats per minute, which translates to more words per minute.

If you were driving along the German autobahn at 90 miles per hour, and your partner suddenly covered your speedometer and asked you to decelerate to 30 miles per hour, at what speed do you think you would 'level off', saying 'That's 30 miles per hour'? Most people estimate between 50 and 60 miles per hour and are correct.

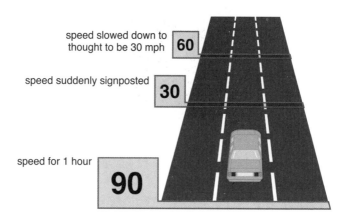

speed slowed down to thought to be 30 mph **60**

speed suddenly signposted **30**

speed for 1 hour **90**

Figure 9.1 Illustration showing how the mind 'gets used to' speed and motion. The same kind of relativistic 'misjudgements' can be used to advantage to help us to learn more adequately.

The reason for this apparent absurdity is that the brain gets used to a new norm and begins to compare all experiences with that norm. This extraordinary ability of your brain to adapt to any new norm is now being used in many areas, including Olympic training. In one instance, runners were attached to a treadmill with a supporting belt. The treadmill was then gradually accelerated past their fastest speed to date, while they were encouraged to keep moving their legs at the appropriate speed. The supporting belt gave them a sense of security. After a series of such training sessions, many of them were able to break their previous records, because their brain/body system had become used to this new, speedier norm.

Increasing your 'beats per minute'

The adjustable nature of your brain can also be applied to improving your reading speed by means of a metronome, which can be used in a number of ways. You can buy a traditional or digital metronome in a music store or download a free one at: **www.webmetronome.com**.

Begin by allowing each beat to indicate a single stroke along the line for your visual guide. In this way, a regular, steady, smooth reading rhythm can be established and maintained, and the usual deceleration in reading speed over time can be avoided. Once you have established a 'possible' reading speed, the metronome beat can be raised one beat per minute and an improvement in your reading speed can be achieved.

A second major use of the metronome is for relativistic speed reading training. In this method of training, you set the metronome at an abnormally high speed, thereby obliging your eye/brain system to become accustomed to a very high new norm. This form of training allows you to 'pull yourself up by the boot straps' by establishing very high new norms. You can then dip below them into comfortably 'slow' reading speeds, which are still twice your previous average.

Below are a series of exercises designed to set you off on the high-speed, high-comprehension path.

EXERCISES

High-speed practise

In the following exercises, use whichever guided reading technique feels most appropriate.

1 Read normally for five minutes from a book that you will be able to continue using. Record your words per minute on your progress graph on pages 222–3.

2 Use any book (light material) of your choice, preferably one in which you are interested.

3 Aim for as much comprehension as possible, but remember that this exercise is concerned primarily with speed. In this exercise, you should continue reading from the last point you reached.
   (a) Practise-read for one minute at 100 wpm faster than your highest normal speed.
   (b) Practise-read 100 wpm faster than (a).
   (c) Practise-read 100 wpm faster than (b).

▶

(d) Practise-read 100 wpm faster than (c).

(e) Practise-read 100 wpm faster than (d) in High-speed practise 1 (below).

(f) Practise-read with comprehension for one minute from the point reached at the end of (e). Calculate and record your wpm on your progress graph on pages 222–3.

5 *High-speed practise 1*

(a) Use any easy book. Start from the beginning of a chapter.

(b) Practise-read with a visual aid, three lines at a time, at a minimum of 2000 wpm for five minutes. Mark the point where you stop.

(c) Re-read to mark in four minutes.

(d) Re-read to mark in three minutes.

(e) Re-read to mark in two minutes.

(f) Read on from mark, for the same comprehension as in (b), for five minutes.

(g) Read for normal comprehension for one minute. Record your wpm on your progress graph on pages 222–3.

6 *High-speed practise 2*

(a) Using any easy book, start at the beginning of a chapter.

(b) Scan for one minute, using a visual aid and taking four seconds per page.

(c) Practise-read from the beginning at a minimum of 2000 wpm for five minutes.

(d) Repeat this exercise when possible.

(e) As 5(g).

7 Exercise your eyes by moving them on horizontal and vertical planes, diagonally upper left to lower right and then upper right to lower left. Speed up gradually, day by day. The purpose of this exercise is to train your eyes to function more accurately and independently.

8 Practise turning 100 pages at approximately two seconds per page, moving your eyes very rapidly down the page. (Do this in two two-minute sessions.)

9 (a) Practise as fast as you can for one minute, not worrying about comprehension.

(b) Read with motivated comprehension for one minute.

(c) Calculate and record your wpm on your progress graph on pages 222–3.

Repeat as time allows.

After you have completed a number of these high-speed practice exercises, go straight to Self-test 5. Before starting the reading proper, it might be an excellent idea to do a two-second-per-page 'metronome sprint' over the whole self-test, as a skim and scan. When you start your actual reading, make sure your brain is especially well set for gathering more information about what you perceived in your 'metronome sprint'.

SELF-TEST 5

Baby brain, by Dr Sue Whiting

The early development of the baby brain is a period of intense neural activity when brain cell interconnections are being forged at a furious pace. It is never too early for the brain to start learning.

Brain spurts
The brain takes longer than any other organ to reach its full development, and its growth pattern is markedly different. In most other organs, basic development is completed in the womb. Further growth in size is through the cellular division as the body grows. The brain, on the other hand, has its full complement of cells before birth – that is why the heads of babies seem out of proportion to the rest of their bodies.

Research carried out during the last ten years builds on previous evidence that the brain begins elaborating on the connections between cells while still in the womb, using spontaneously generated signals. At about eight weeks after conception, the first of the 'brain spurts' begins (the term 'brain spurt' relates to increased development of the brain). Over the next five weeks the majority of nerve cells are formed. The second 'brain spurt' begins approximately ten weeks before birth and continues for about two years after birth. The second spurt is a period of intense activity for the brain cells: interconnections are refined, tuned and expanded. This increase in connectivity results in a rapid growth of the brain. At birth it weighs 25 per cent of its adult weight, at six months it is 50 per cent, at two and a half years 75 per cent and at five years 90 per cent.

Introduction to the world

Studies have shown that a child responds positively and specifically to the tones of the human voice at birth. A high-speed film of a newborn baby, when slowed down and examined frame by frame, shows that tiny gestures on the part of the child are synchronised with specific tones and syllables from the parent(s). Sounds other than the human voice produce no such response. This implies that some linguistic skills are learnt while in the womb. Having heard the mother's heart while in the womb, this sound is recognised by the baby and has a soothing effect.

Tom Bower's research on infant perception at the University of Edinburgh shows that a child experiences a three-dimensional world from birth. Using polarising goggles so that the left and right eye see different images, he created the visual illusion that there was a solid object in front of the baby. Bower found that even newborn babies stretched out their hands to touch the apparent object, but as soon as their hand closed upon empty air instead of a solid object the baby started crying. This shows that at birth a child expects visual objects to be tangible, and indicates a simple unity of the visual and tactile senses.

Sight and sound

Other experiments at Edinburgh have shown that sight and sound are also integrated, the newborn turning its head in the direction of a sound, especially the mother's voice. They have shown that a baby is also born with the ability to recognise smells as pleasant or unpleasant, turning its head toward or away as appropriate.

The newborn child can also recognise a human face. Robert Frantz, a researcher at Western Reserve University in Cleveland, presented day-old children with the choice of looking at a picture of a face, a bull's eye, newsprint, or coloured circles. He found a preference for the human face, most of the babies looking at it far more than the other objects. Mark Johnson, of Carnegie Mellion, carried out similar tests on infants as young as ten minutes; and observed a marked preference for pictures of faces to pictures of blank ovals or faces with scrambled features. This implies, according to Johnson, that humans are born with a 'template' of a face which helps us to discern the source of food, warmth and protection.

Babies who are spoken to as human beings, rather than just cooed at, have a much greater opportunity to pick up language. A rich early environment, where one or both parents consciously aim to develop their child's sensory experience, can speed up and enhance development. As early as 1952, Aaron Stern decided his daughter, Edith, could benefit from a consciously stimulating environment. From birth, he talked to her as much as possible (not baby talk), played classical music, and showed her flash cards with numbers and animals on them. This technique has been adapted and used by countless other parents, with very positive results.

Ramps, ladders and wheels

To assess the effect of a rich environment on brain growth, Mark Rosenweig, at the University of California at Berkeley, allowed a group of baby rats to grow up in a cage full of ramps, ladders, wheels, tunnels and other stimuli. A second group was left in barren cages. After 105 days the brains were examined, showing the brains of the rats raised in the rich environment to have more connections than the control group. There were also 15 per cent more cells, and the neurone bodies were 15 per cent larger, and, perhaps most importantly, there were more interconnections with other neurones.

The belief in biologically programmed core knowledge lies at the heart of most baby development research, not only with mathematics and physics, but with other cognitive skills. Just when such core knowledge is programmed is as yet uncertain. Since 1988, when a special multi-electrode device was invented at the California Institute of Technology, it has been possible to detect and measure cells in the brains of mammal foetuses firing impulses to each other, making, tuning and adapting connections while in the womb. Work carried out on such neural activity suggests that it is during the 'brain spurts' that the interconnections are developed, rather than each neural connection being stored in our genes. Given the millions of connections which need to be formed in the brain, the former theory would need much less genetic information to be stored. It would imply that genetic blueprints are worked on as the baby is in the womb and during infancy.

Nature versus nurture

The above is a relatively new hypothesis. Much work needs to be carried out to develop and demonstrate it. It would add a vital new insight into the nature and nurture debate.

▶

In a field of research which involves a multitude of theories, studies and conclusions, revelations of the potential of babies given the right stimuli will continue to encourage parents. The vital influence of nurture gives all parents the chance to help their offspring as much as they can, in whatever way they see fit and feasible.

Whether due to genetic programming, or whether due to the interconnections made between neurones while still in the womb and during the critical first few months, our awareness of babies' mental abilities and capabilities is growing. Whatever ways parents find to encourage and enhance their children's mental development, two key points must be considered.

First, continuity must be observed. A child whose abilities are more developed than those of his or her schoolmates may deliberately hold back, in order not to appear different or to avoid jealous derision.

Secondly, care must be taken to truly respect the developing child's wishes and interests. Having invested a lot of time, emotion and hopes, parents must be aware of not putting too much control on how the fruits of their labour are used. The main issue is the happiness and fulfilment of the child, and the joy of parenting lies in taking an active part.

STOP YOUR TIMER NOW!

Length of time: _____ mins

Next, calculate your reading speed in words per minute (wpm) by simply dividing the number of words in the passage (in this case, 1260) by the time (in minutes) you took.

$$\textbf{Words per minute (wpm)} = \frac{\textbf{number of words}}{\textbf{time}}$$

When you have completed your calculation, enter the number in the words per minute (wpm) slot at the end of this paragraph, and also enter it on your progress graph and chart on pages 222–3.

Words per minute: _____

Self-test 5: Comprehension

1 The human brain:
   (a) has a full complement of cells at conception
   (b) has a full complement of cells before birth
   (c) has a full complement of cells one month after birth
   (d) has a full complement of cells two years after birth

2 The first of the 'brain spurts' begins:
   (a) at conception
   (b) eight weeks after conception
   (c) four months after conception
   (d) one month before birth

3 The second 'brain spurt' begins approximately:
   (a) eight weeks after conception
   (b) ten weeks after conception
   (c) ten weeks before birth
   (d) four weeks before birth

4 At birth the human brain weighs what percentage of its adult weight?
   (a) 10 per cent
   (b) 15 per cent
   (c) 25 per cent
   (d) 40 per cent

5 At six months the brain weighs what percentage of its adult weight?
   (a) 25 per cent
   (b) 40 per cent
   (c) 50 per cent
   (d) 75 per cent

6 At two and a half years the brain weighs what percentage of its adult weight?
   (a) 50 per cent
   (b) 75 per cent
   (c) 80 per cent
   (d) 90 per cent

7 At five years the human brain weighs what percentage of its adult weight?

(a) 85 per cent
(b) 90 per cent
(c) 95 per cent
(d) 100 per cent

8 The human baby can respond positively and specifically
  to tones of the human voice on the day of its birth.   *True/False*

9 Tom Bower's research on infant perception at the University of
  Edinburgh shows that at birth a child:
  (a) sees only blurred images
  (b) immediately focuses on its mother
  (c) can hear sounds well
  (d) experiences a three-dimensional world immediately

10 Other experiments at Edinburgh have shown that sight and sound are
   also integrated, a newborn turning its head in the direction of the sound,
   especially _____

11 Robert Frantz and Mark Johnson discovered that a newborn child
   showed a marked preference for pictures of:
   (a) its mother
   (b) coloured circles
   (c) faces
   (d) animals

12 Children who are 'cooed' at have a much greater
   opportunity to pick up language.   *True/False*

13 Mark Rosenweig's experiments with rats showed that those in an
   enriched environment:
   (a) had smaller brains
   (b) grew physically bigger
   (c) had no changes in their brain
   (d) had more connections between brain cells

14 Neural interconnections are developed in the baby's brain:
   (a) during 'brain spurts'

(b) before birth

(c) from storage compartments in our genes

(d) during the first two years of life

15 The main issue in parenting is:

(a) developing a genius

(b) providing a good academic education

(c) the happiness and fulfilment of the child

(d) not interfering with the child's natural development

Check your answers against those on page 216. Then divide your score by 15 and multiply by 100 to calculate your percentage comprehension.

Comprehension score: _____ out of 15

_____ per cent

Now enter your score on your progress graph and chart on pages 222–3.

Armed with information about the astonishing range of abilities and sophistication of your eyes, and with techniques for getting the maximum benefit from your eye/brain system, you are ready to tackle the main 'problem areas' in reading, namely lack of concentration, lack of comprehension, as well as the various, usually misnamed, 'learning difficulty' syndromes.

I am not a **speed reader**.

I am a **speed understander**.

SCIENTIST AND SCIENCE FICTION AUTHOR
ISAAC ASIMOV

Part 3
Overcome your reading hurdles

In this part we explore the barriers to concentration and comprehension – typically sub-vocalisation, finger-pointing, regression and back-skipping – and how to overcome them. Once a problem is faced, analysed and understood, it becomes a positive energy centre for the creation of solutions. I believe *all* reading problems and learning difficulties can be dealt with and the situation improved. In most cases the problems can be completely overcome. This part also shows you how to develop advanced speed reading skills and to master and massively increase your vocabulary using mnemonic devices to remember prefixes, suffixes and roots.

Troubleshooting common reading problems

This chapter discusses some of the most frequently mentioned reading problems – sub-vocalisation, finger-pointing,
regression and back-skipping – which are all major barriers
to efficient reading. New approaches, based on research on
the functioning and relationship of the eye and brain, are
offered to correct much of what has been written on these
subjects. In addition, this chapter deals with the two most
common 'learning difficulty' areas: dyslexia and attention
deficit/hyperactivity disorder (ADHD)/attention disability disorder syndrome (ADDS) (also known as attention deficit
disorder syndrome).

Sub-vocalisation

A common reading 'problem' is sub-vocalisation, the tendency to
mouth the words you are reading. It is caused by the way in which
children are taught to read: usually by the phonetic or phonic
method or the look–say method (as discussed on pages 1–2).

Almost every book and course on speed reading maintains that
this habit is one of the greatest barriers to improvement and that it

must be overcome. However, the truth of the matter is that all of us can *benefit* from sub-vocalisation. In the real sense of the word, sub-vocalisation cannot and should not be completely eliminated. Once this is understood, the 'problem' may be approached in its proper perspective, leading to much more satisfactory reading habits. People who are instructed to eliminate sub-vocalisation often become discouraged and lose their enjoyment of reading altogether after spending weeks attempting to accomplish the impossible.

The proper approach to this problem is to accept that, while sub-vocalisation always persists, it can be pushed further and further back into the semi-conscious. In other words, while never being able to eliminate the habit completely, you can become less dependent upon it. This means that you need not worry when you occasionally realise that you are sub-vocalising, because it is a universal habit.

The positive side to sub-vocalisation is that you can actually *use* it as an aid to remembering what you have read. Assuming that practice has enabled you to become less dependent on sub-vocalisation, you can consciously increase the volume of your sub-vocalisation when reading important words or concepts (shouting them internally), thus making those bits of information stand out from the rest.

In addition sub-vocalisation is not, by definition, a slow, plodding process. It is quite possible for your brain to sub-vocalise as many as 2000 words per minute. Indeed, there are now a number of people who can speak at above 1000 words per minute. So only start worrying about sub-vocalisation, if it is your choice to worry, when you reach these speeds!

Finger-pointing

Traditionally considered a problem because of our misconception that it slows the reader down, finger-pointing is in fact (as we have seen in Chapter 4) an excellent method of maintaining concentration and focus. The only disadvantage is that the physical size of the finger and hand block the view. Thus, the 'problem' suggests the solution – the use of a slim guide making the habit a perfect one for accelerated reading speeds.

Regression and back-skipping

These are two similar but distinct 'problems'. Regression is a conscious returning to words, phrases or paragraphs that you feel you have missed or misunderstood. Many readers are urged to return to them in order to understand the material. Back-skipping is a kind of visual tic, an unconscious skipping back to words or phrases that you have just read. You are almost never aware that you are back-skipping.

As outlined in Chapter 4, back-skipping and regression add to the number of fixations per line, slowing down the reading process. Both these habits are usually unnecessary. Studies performed on the conscious re-reading of material indicate that readers who were sure they needed to return to certain words or sections in order to understand them showed little change in their comprehension scores when not allowed to do so. It is not so much a matter of comprehension as of having confidence in your brain's ability.

The approach to eliminating or reducing these two habits is twofold.

1 First, you must force yourself not to re-read sections that you think you may have missed.

2 Second, you must gradually push up your speed, trying to maintain an even rhythm in your eye movements.

3 Both speed and rhythm will make back-skipping and regression more difficult, while actually improving your comprehension.

These 'problem' areas described above may now no longer be seen as the major barriers that so many people have made them out to be. They are simply habits that can be adjusted and, in many cases, used to great advantage.

Dealing with dyslexia

'Dyslexia' is a term commonly applied to a person who has difficulty in decoding letters of the alphabet and consequently in reading words. People with dyslexia often get letters reversed and tend to have scrawly handwriting. In some schools and school districts, more than 20 per cent of children are labelled with this 'learning disability'.

In my own experience, more than 80 per cent of those people I have met who have been labelled dyslexic are not. They have simply stumbled at one of the many early stages of their reading career and never been allowed to get up. To realise how easy it is to fall at an early stage, imagine that you are a Martian. You land, completely innocently, on the planet Earth. Someone rapidly explains to you that these particular space beings have a series of random shapes that they call letters and that they put into words. Just to make things more difficult, many of the shapes are incredibly similar.

To understand how difficult the task is, try the following exercise. Rapidly point to each of the different shapes in Figure 10.1, moving from one to the next as fast as you can, naming them accurately as you go. Most people find that, sooner or later, they stumble and misidentify one of them.

Figure 10.1 Hard-to-learn shapes that can result in a misdiagnosis of dyslexia in the beginning reader.

You are now back as a Martian, having been told the names of these various squiggles, and you are asked to write the word 'god'. You search your memory banks and vaguely remember that the three letters probably have a circle in them. Writing down three circles, 'ooo', you then also vaguely remember that there seemed to be an upward stick and a downward stick somewhere in there; on the first circle you put an upward stick on the right-hand side of the circle, and on the last circle you put a downward stick, also on the right-hand side. Confidently believing that you are nearly if not perfectly correct, you hand in your paper, only to be greeted with derision and the statement that you are probably dyslexic – or, to put it more brutally, suffering from some minor form of brain damage. (You have in fact arranged the word 'dog'.) This would obviously put you into a particularly tense frame of mind, increasing the probability that you would make a mistake on your next attempt.

This scenario is precisely what has happened to many people labelled dyslexic, and all because, in the beginning, they were not given the tools necessary for memory – namely *association* and *image* – which would have enabled them to recall the names of the letters easily. Their first mistake fitted into the definition of dyslexia and they were falsely labelled, entering a downward spiral that made them get worse as their academic careers progressed.

Very often the person labelled dyslexic tries to read more slowly and carefully in order to gain better comprehension, thereby unwittingly making the problem even worse. If you have ever been labelled dyslexic, the following two stories may give you hope.

A 16-year-old girl in the Scandinavian School of Brussels attended a Buzan Centre course on Mind Mapping and Learning. On the first day she did exceptionally well. On the morning of the second day she came up to the teacher and asked to be excused from the morning session: it was on speed reading and she couldn't read very well at all because she was 'dyslexic' and because, as she put it, 'I can't really read properly'. The teacher encouraged her to give it a try, which she did. The result? From an initial reading speed of 100 words per minute and poor comprehension, she graduated at the end of the day with a speed of 600 words per minute and 70 per cent comprehension.

The second story concerns a script editor who described her school years as 'sheer hell'. Having failed to learn reading properly at school, she had been utterly devastated, because she loved reading and literature. Being of a persistent frame of mind, she stuck to her reading tasks, working extra hours at a pace at least four times as slow as her contemporaries.

Her dream had always been to be a script editor, a job that she finally managed to acquire. However, after six months, she was beginning to sink because she had to spend not only her full working day but also most of the night working through her reading material in order to keep up with the pace demanded by the job.

Like the Scandinavian girl, the script editor started with a reading speed of 100 words per minute and very poor comprehension. Throughout the course she had kept her 'secret' private. At the end of the final reading test, she had increased her speed to 700 words per minute with good comprehension. She stood up the instant she had calculated her final speed and told her story. Everyone had expected her to be thrilled, but she was trembling from head to foot.

She explained that, for her entire life, she had been embarrassed by her incompetence and inability and that suddenly all that was disappearing: it was cause for celebration. At the same time, however, she was experiencing an almost uncontrollable fury about her wasted years, her lifetime of humiliation, and her sudden realisation that the dyslexic label had abused her and kept her in a mental prison. And all of it unnecessary.

The happy ending to the story is that the script editor returned to her job and was able to complete her daily tasks in fewer than normal working hours.

As I have said, many people labelled dyslexic are not actually dyslexic, and even if they are the fundamental solution to their reading problems is the same: use a guide, gradually accelerate the speed, and escape the semantic prison of sentences by using Mind Maps as a note-taking and thinking device. (For more on Mind Mapping, see *The Mind Map Book* and visit **www.imindmap.com**.) At the time of writing, neither I nor any of my teachers have found anyone, either falsely or correctly labelled as dyslexic, who was not able to improve their reading speed and comprehension significantly.

ADDS/ADHD and hyperactivity

A great deal of controversy surrounds ADDS/ADHD. One terrifying statistic confirms that, in the USA alone, over three million children have been diagnosed as having the disorder so seriously that they are on the drug methylphenidate hydrochloride (Ritalin®).

The debate rages as to whether the syndrome exists as a medically definable illness, whether it is a dangerous generalised diagnosis made by ignorant doctors, whether teachers are sticking the ADDS/ADHD labels on children as a cover-up for their own inability to maintain the child's interest, and whether Ritalin is a miracle drug or one that is normalising, numbing and drugging fundamentally active and creative children into a conformist stupor.

To help you draw your own conclusions, the following information may prove useful.

ADHD is defined, by the American Psychiatric Association and others as a classifiable illness if an individual meets eight or more of the following criteria:

- Cannot remain seated if required to do so

- Easily distracted by external stimuli

- Experiences difficulty focusing on a single task or play activity

- Frequently begins another activity without completing the first (it is interesting to note that Leonardo da Vinci, normally regarded as one of the greatest geniuses of all time, was consistently accused of this)

- Fidgets or squirms (or feels restless mentally)

- Can't (or doesn't want to) wait for his or her turn during group activities

- Often interrupts with an answer before a question is completed

- Has problems with chores or following through on a job

- Likes to make noises while playing

- Interrupts others inappropriately

- Talks impulsively or excessively

- Doesn't seem to listen when spoken to by a teacher

- Impulsively jumps into physically dangerous activities

- Regularly loses things (pencils, tools, papers) necessary to complete school work projects.

These forms of behaviour must have commenced before the age of seven years and must occur more frequently than in the average person of the same age. This means that at least half the population will, by definition, exhibit these forms of behaviour more frequently than the average. Are they all therefore suffering from an illness?

Two classic cases are worth bearing in mind:

As a young girl, Mary-Lou Retton was so superactive that her parents were advised to put her on a course of drugs that would dramatically reduce her physical activity. Fortunately, her parents were of a different opinion and requested that the school find ways of using her extraordinary energy more appropriately. Thirteen years later, Mary-Lou Retton, internationally renowned for her boundless enthusiasm, easily won the gold medal in women's gymnastics at the Los Angeles Olympics.

A few years before Mary-Lou experienced her difficulties in her early school years, a little boy named Daley Thompson was experiencing the same problems in England. Similarly, his parents were encouraged to put him on a course of tranquillising drugs. Like Mary-Lou's parents, Daley's insisted that he be given exercises and activities that would absorb his ebullience. Daley proved virtually indefatigable, wearing out every physical education teacher available. It all paid off wonderfully well when Daley Thompson became the world and Olympic decathlon champion and stayed at the peak of his sport, shattering all previous world records consistently, for ten years.

Thom Hartmann, in his excellent book *Attention Deficit Disorder: A Different Perception*, is firmly of the opinion that the labels are often wildly inappropriate. Hartmann claims that schools are set up for the 'farmers' – those who will sit at a desk, watch and listen attentively to the teacher, and always do what they are told. This is the ultimate torture for the 'hunters', who are physically active, always scanning their environment, creative, impulsive, and always looking – like Leonardo da Vinci – for the next exciting event.

Whether or not you think you suffer from dyslexia or hyperactivity, there are some general pointers that will allow you to concentrate and comprehend more easily – and these are highlighted in the next chapter.

Improving your concentration and comprehension

Having tackled some basic reading problems, we are now ready to discuss what causes poor concentration and comprehension and suggest ways to tackle such shortcomings. When you maintain concentration, your eye/brain system becomes laser-like in its ability to focus and absorb.

The importance of reading goals

An interesting example of one of the great historical geniuses applying his enormous concentration powers to the task of reading is that of President Thomas Jefferson, widely regarded as the greatest all-round intellect ever produced by the USA. Professor Robert Zorn reports that Jefferson believed in mapping out his reading into a definite plan of action, defining specific goals for each topic that he covered, and never allowing himself to deviate from his reading schedule until he had completed the task. No distractions and no dissipation of time by 'scattered inattentiveness' were the keys to Jefferson's methodology and to his unparalleled powers of concentration. Jefferson offered this very modern-sounding advice to the reader: you should know 'where you are, and what you are doing, and what time it is, and whether you are falling short of your schedule or not, and, if so, how far short.' This chapter will enable you to approach Jefferson's extraordinary concentration and comprehension levels.

What causes poor concentration?

The many reasons for lack of concentration when reading include:

- vocabulary difficulties;
- conceptual difficulty of the material;
- inappropriate reading speed;
- incorrect mind set;
- poor organisation;
- lack of interest;
- lack of motivation.

Vocabulary difficulties

Once you have increased your vocabulary with the information and exercises in Part 4, you will already be on the way to solving this one. In addition, if the material you are reading continually confronts you with words that you do not understand or that you understand only vaguely, your concentration will gradually become worse because the ideas you are trying to absorb will be interrupted by gaps in understanding. A smooth inflow of information, unhampered by the lurking fear of misunderstanding, is a necessity for efficient reading. The vocabulary analysis and exercises in this book are designed to overcome this difficulty.

If you do come to a word that you do not understand, just underline it and read on. Usually the meaning becomes vaguely apparent from the context of the sentence. Then, at the end of the chapter or that day's reading, you can do a 'dictionary run' and look up all the unknown words at the same time.

Conceptual difficulty of the material

This is a slightly more difficult problem to overcome and usually arises in academic books. The best approach is to 'multiple read' the material using the guided reading techniques as well as skimming, scanning, paragraph structure and previewing (the latter are discussed in Chapters 7 and 14).

Inappropriate reading speed

This is often a product of the school system. When children are given important or difficult material, they are usually told: 'Read this slowly and carefully.' This approach establishes a vicious circle: the more slowly you read, the less you understand, which makes the material seem even more incomprehensible. Ultimately, a point of complete frustration is reached and the material is often abandoned in despair.

If you have poor concentration and comprehension, this may well be the problem, so vary your speeds on difficult material, trying to go faster rather than more slowly, and you may find a great improvement. By learning to speed and range read, you will have control and choice of the appropriate speed for the material, needs, time of day, energy level, and internal and external environments.

Incorrect mind set

This simply means that your mind has not really been directed in the best way towards the material you are trying to read. You may, for instance, still be concentrating on an argument that took place in the office or a social engagement for the coming evening.

What you must try to do is to shake out the unnecessary threads that are running through your mind and then direct yourself to thinking actively about the subject you are reading. You may even go so far as to stop for a moment and consciously gather together your thoughts. One way to do this most efficiently is to do a rapid two-minute Mind Map (see *The Mind Map Book*) on the topic you are studying in order to recollect your thoughts and to provide you with an even stronger ongoing mental set.

Poor organisation

This problem is far more common than many people realise. Actually getting down to reading a book is a battle of the will and almost demands a run-up to the desk in order to gain enough impetus actually to sit down at it. Having arrived and started to read, many people suddenly realise that they don't have a pencil, notepaper, their glasses and any number of other things. Consequently, they then disrupt their concentration to get these materials. The solution is easy: before you sit down to read, make sure that all the materials you will need are readily available.

Lack of interest

This is a problem most often experienced by students or people taking special courses, and we devote extra attention to it in our reading courses. The first step in solving this problem is to review the points discussed in this chapter, for lack of interest is often related to other difficulties. For instance, interest will be difficult to maintain if a deficient vocabulary is continually interrupting understanding, if the material is confusing, if other thoughts keep popping up, and if the necessary materials are not available.

Assuming that these problems are overcome and that your interest is still not as high as it should be, you need to analyse your personal approach to the material. First, make sure that the technique being used is appropriate. If this fails, you can try the 'severe critic' approach: rather than reading the material as you normally would, get annoyed at it for having presented you with problems and try to analyse it thoroughly, concentrating especially on the negative aspects. You will find yourself actually becoming interested in the material, much in the way that you become interested in listening to the arguments of someone whom you don't particularly like and wish to oppose vigorously.

Lack of motivation

This is a different problem, often stemming from having no clearly defined purpose to your reading. Once you have analysed your

reasons for reading the book or article, your motivation may automatically increase. Alternatively, you may conclude that you need
not read it at all. If your reasons are valid, there may indeed be no
point in reading the book – but make sure they are really valid.

Harnessing your concentration

In my 30 years of lecturing around the world on speed reading
skills, I have found that 99.9 per cent of people admit to having
problems with concentration. This problem regularly manifests itself
in periods of day-dreaming, which occur at least once every 30–40
minutes. Once again, our inappropriate training has made us see
something that is actually good in a bad light. When your brain day-
dreams after 30 or 40 minutes, it is doing exactly what it should –
taking a break at exactly the right time. So, in most cases, it is not a
question of losing concentration but rather a more positive matter
of taking a break when you should.

Let us, though, examine what actually happens when you 'lose
concentration' while reading a book: what actually happens is that
you concentrate on a few pages of the book, after which you concentrate on someone walking by, after which you concentrate on a
few more lines or pages of the book, after which you concentrate
on a bird landing on a tree outside your window, after which you
concentrate on the book again, after which you concentrate on your
fingernail, after which you concentrate on the book again, after
which you concentrate on a day-dream, after which you concentrate on the book once more.

Throughout the entire period you have been *concentrating*! The
problem is not with your concentration, for you are concentrating
100 per cent of the time. The problem is with the direction and
focus of that perfect concentration. Concentration can thus be seen
as a wild stallion, with you as the rider. In most instances, the stallion has its way, going off at full gallop in whatever direction it
pleases. As a masterful rider/reader, it is up to you to rein in the
stallion of your concentration, steering it in the direction appropriate
to the reading task at hand.

So, remember to take breaks every 30–60 minutes in order to improve concentration and give your eyes and brain a needed rest. When you return to reading, check that your reading speeds are appropriate to the material you are reading. Again, make sure you are following the appropriate goals you set out before you started to read, and check that your environment is appropriately organised for your reading task.

Now that your visual skills are rapidly improving, and your concentration stallion is under your control, you are ready to move on to Part 4 – Mastermind Your Speed Reading Skills. In this part, you will learn the art and technique of previewing which allows you to develop a structure to see the whole text 'to view' before delving into the detail. You will also be given the major keys to unlock your vocabulary power – one of the prime factors in overall reading success. Then you will discover how speed reading can be applied equally effectively to literature and poetry as it can be to information and study. Finally you will learn how to speed read printed and online information and avoid information overload.

What you have been **learning** and will **continue to learn** throughout these pages is an **entire range of reading skills** from which you can pick the appropriate **individual item** or **combination of items** to **revolutionize** your reading process – and **change your life!**

TONY BUZAN

Part 4

Mastermind your speed reading skills

Since 1966 I have taught the fundamental principles of speed and range reading in more than 50 countries, to students ranging from three-year-old children to chief executives of multinational corporations. In every country, regardless of age and status, similar questions arise. These include:

- 'I can see how you would use this for other subjects, but you couldn't really use it for the sciences, could you?'
- 'You wouldn't apply speed and range reading to the appreciation of literature and poetry, would you?'
- 'You surely wouldn't preview a detective story!'
- 'On really difficult material, you'd have to read slowly, wouldn't you?'
- 'Surely you wouldn't use speed and range reading if you were reading for relaxation and pleasure?'

Intriguingly, the answer is that your growing knowledge can be applied to *all* of these situations. From now on, every page of every book you read will be approached slightly differently from every other page, and you will be to the printed word as a dolphin is to water. Part 4 gives you more detailed information on advanced applications.

The art of previewing

'Preview' means just what it says: you break the word into its component parts and pre-view – see before. When you allow your brain to see the whole text beforehand you navigate far more effectively on your second run-through. The purpose of the preview is to develop a structure into which your mind can more easily fit the smaller details of that structure, thus immediately improving your comprehension of the whole.

Scouting for words

The previewer can be likened to a 'mind reconnaissance scout' who goes ahead of the troops to determine the lie of the land, the position of the enemy forces and areas of tactical advantage. It is easier for an army to manoeuvre and operate in unknown territory if it has major reference points; in the same way, it is easier for the mind to attack or understand information once it has major landmarks by which to go.

Previewing should be applied to whatever kind of material you are going to read, whether it be letters, reports, reference works, novels or articles. In all cases, it will speed up your overall reading and will improve your understanding because you will no longer be stumbling over items one after the other but instead will be fitting pieces into a general picture.

Your approach to the preview should combine the elements of skimming with what you have learnt about paragraph structure. In other words, you will sensibly and rapidly go over the material you are about to read, selecting those areas most likely to hold the major chunks of information. When you are previewing, always use your favourite guiding technique. The concept of previewing as described here is for use in your general reading.

Strategies for previewing

Playing the following active reading games will guarantee that your mental set is more appropriate, that your brain/eye system is searching for the best information as you preview, and that the whole process becomes more fun.

Apply what you already know

When you apply what you already know, you will often find that you know more than you thought. Many people incorrectly assume that the author is the expert, when in fact very often the reader knows as much as or more than the author. Always quickly Mind Map your knowledge of the subject just before you read a new book. You can then use this knowledge to make new associations from the book and to ask appropriate questions.

Interact actively with the author

When you read a book, it should be a conversation between you and the brain that created the book, not a one-way lecture. It is most important that you interact with whatever text you read by noting down questions or comments in the margin of the book or on a separate piece of paper.

Be a detective

Constantly try to predict what is going to happen next in the text, what 'plan of action' the author had. Keep trying to be one step ahead in solving the puzzle of the information you are absorbing.

Preview everything you read for the next two weeks, checking how much knowledge you gain from each preview and how much more effectively it enables you to understand when you are reading the material for the second time. Practise the previewing techniques you have learnt on a book, while at the same time using an advanced guiding technique to read the entire book in less than ten minutes.

One of the obstacles to effective speed reading is having a limited vocabulary. The next chapter shows you how to expand your knowledge of words beyond what you ever thought possible.

Mastermind your vocabulary

Having dealt with the workings of the eye/brain system, the theory behind eye movements and the major problem areas in reading, we now move on to vocabulary. The average person's conversational vocabulary is about 1000 words; the number of available words is over a million. Of our three vocabularies (conversational, written and recognition), recognition is the largest. Improving your vocabulary raises your intelligence. This chapter introduces you to three kinds of vocabulary and provides key lists of prefixes, suffixes and roots that will give you access to the meanings of thousands of words.

The importance of vocabulary

The extent of one's vocabulary is an indication of the amount of material that one has been able to assimilate and read. Schools, colleges and universities therefore include general vocabulary testing as one of the major criteria by which they judge the suitability of applicants, and the success or failure of students often depends on their ability to understand and use words properly.

The importance of vocabulary extends, of course, far beyond the academic world: the businessperson who has at their command a wider range of words than their peers is at an immediate advantage; and the person who, in social situations, can both understand easily and comment creatively also has the upper hand.

Our three kinds of vocabulary

Most of us have more than one vocabulary; in fact, we usually have at least three. First is the vocabulary we use in conversation, and in many cases this may not exceed 1000 words (even though it is estimated that the English language contains well over a million words).

Our second vocabulary is the one we use when writing. This tends to be larger than the spoken one, because more time is devoted to the construction and content of sentences and because there is less pressure on the writer.

The largest of the three is our recognition vocabulary – the words that we understand and appreciate when we hear them in conversation or when we read them, but that we ourselves may not use either in writing or in conversation. Ideally, of course, both our speaking and our writing vocabulary should be as large as our recognition vocabulary, but in practice this is seldom the case. It is possible, however, to increase all three quite dramatically.

The power of prefixes

The purpose of this chapter is to introduce you to over 80 prefixes (letters, syllables or words placed at the beginning of a word). Many of them are concerned with position, opposition and movement. As the English language has a large element of Greek and Latin, many of the prefixes are from these two languages.

Just to give you some idea of the incredible power of these basic units of vocabulary, Dr Minninger of the University of Minnesota has estimated that 14 of these alone offer the keys to over 14,000 word meanings. She further confirms that, by the age of 25 years, the average person's vocabulary development has become almost moribund. It is 95 per cent complete, leaving a mere 5 per cent to be added over the possible 75 years of life that still remain. The 14 prefixes and roots listed below were found in over 14,000 words from a standard desktop dictionary and were found in roughly 100,000 words from a large unabridged dictionary.

These 'mini power words' have been extracted from the larger lists for you. As you read through this chapter, be on the look-out for them, as well as absorbing all the others.

14 words containing key prefixes

Word	Prefix	Common meaning	Root	Common meaning
Precept	pre-	before	capere	take, seize
Detain	de-	away, down	tenere	hold, have
Intermittent	inter-	between, among	mittere	send
Offer	ob-	against	ferre	bear, carry
Insist	in-	into	stare	stand
Monograph	mono-	alone, one	graphein	write
Epilogue	epi-	upon	logos	speech, study of
Advance	ad-	to, towards	specere	see
Uncomplicated	un-	not	plicare	fold
	com-	together, with		
Non-extended	non-	not	tendere	stretch
	ex-	out, beyond		
Reproduction	re-	back, again	ducere	lead
	pro-	forward, for		
Indisposed	in-	not	ponere	put, place
	dis-	apart, not		
Over-sufficient	over-	above	facere	make, do
	sub-	under		
Mistranscribe	mis-	wrong	scribere	write
	trans-	across, beyond		

Study the following table thoroughly; it will give you the key to thousands of unfamiliar words. For a method of perfectly memorising this and the other vocabulary lists, refer to *The Memory Book*.

85 prefixes

Prefix	Meaning	Example
a-, an- (G)	without, not	anaerobic
ab-, abs- (L)	away, from, apart	absent
ad-, ac-, af- (L)	to, towards	advent, advance
aero-	air	aeroplane, aeronaut
amb-, ambi- (G)	both, around	ambiguous
amphi- (G)	both, around	amphitheatre
ante- (L)	before	antenatal
anti- (G)	against	antidote, antitoxic
apo- (G)	away from	apostasy
arch- (G)	chief, most important	archbishop, arch-criminal
auto- (G)	self	automatic, autocrat
be-	about, make	belittle, beguile, beset
bene- (L)	well, good	benediction
bi- (G)	two	biennial, bicycle
by-, bye- (G)	added to	byway, bye-law
cata- (G)	down	catalogue, cataract
centi-, cente- (L)	hundred	centigrade, centenary
circum- (L)	around	circumference, circumambient
co-, col-, com-, cor-, con- (L)	together, with	companion, collect, cooperate
contra- (L)	against, counter	contradict, contraceptive
de- (F)	down	denude, decentralise
deca-, deci- (G)	ten	decade, decagon
demi- (L)	half	demigod
dia- (G)	through, between	diameter
dis- (L)	not, opposite to	dislike, disagree
duo- (G)	two	duologue, duplex
dys- (G)	ill, hard	dysentery

The Speed Reading Book

e-, ex-	out of	exhale, excavate
ec- (L)	out of	eccentric
en-, in-, em-, im- (L, G, F)	into, not	enrage, inability, emulate, impress
epi- (G)	upon, at, in addition	epidemic, epidermis
equi-	equally	equidistant
extra- (L)	outside, beyond	extramarital
for-, fore- (E)	before	foresee
hemi- (G)	half	hemisphere
hepta- (G)	seven	heptagon
hexa- (G)	six	hexagon, hexateuch
homo- (L)	same	homonym
hyper- (G)	above, excessive	hypercritical, hypertrophy
il-	not	illegal, illogical
in-, im- (un-) (L, G, F)	not	imperfect, inaccessible
inter- (L)	among, between	interrupt, intermarriage
intra-, intro- (L)	inside, within	intramural, introvert
iso- (G)	equal, same	isobaric, isosceles
mal- (L)	bad, wrong	malfunction, malformed
meta- (G)	after, beyond	metabolism, metaphysical
mis-	wrongly	misfit, mislead
mono- (G)	one, single	monotonous, monocular
multi- (L)	many	multipurpose, multimillion
non-	not	nonsense, nonpareil
ob-, oc-, of-, op- (L)	in the way of, resistance	obstruct, obstacle, oppose
octa-, octo- (G)	eight	octahedron, octave
off-	away, apart	offset
out-	beyond	outnumber, outstanding
over-	above	overhear, overcharge
para- (G)	aside, beyond	parable, paradox

Prefix	Meaning	Example
penta- (G)	five	pentagon, pentateuch
per- (L)	through	perennial, peradventure
peri- (G)	around, about	perimeter, pericardium
poly- (G)	many	polygamy, polytechnic
post- (L)	after	postscript, postnatal
pre- (L)	before	prehistoric, pre-war
prime-, primo- (L)	first, important	primary, prime minister
pro- (L)	in front of, favouring	prologue, pro-British
quadri- (L)	four	quadrennial, quadrangle
re- (L)	again, back	reappear, recivilise
retro- (L)	backward	retrograde, retrospect
se-	aside	secede
self-	personalising	self-control, self-taught
semi- (G)	half	semicircle, semidetached
sub- (L)	under	submarine, subterranean
super- (L)	above, over	superfluous, superior
syl-	with, together	syllogism
syn-, sym- (G)	together	sympathy, synchronise
tele- (G)	far, at or to a distance	telegram, telepathy
ter- (L)	three times	tercentenary
tetra- (G)	four	tetrahedron, tetralogy
trans- (L)	across, through	transatlantic, translate
tri- (L, G)	three	triangle, tripartite
ultra- (L)	beyond	ultramarine, ultraviolet
un- (im-) (L, G, F)	not	unbroken, unbutton, unable
under-	below	underfed, underling
uni- (L)	one	unicellular, uniform
vice- (L)	in place of	viceroy, vice-president
yester- (E)	preceding time	yesterday, yesteryear

E, English, F, French, G, Greek, L, Latin.

Vocabulary mastermind

The following exercises are not vocabulary tests in the strict sense. In many cases, definitions have been 'stretched' a little in order to include a key word that carries an appropriate prefix.

At the top of each vocabulary exercise there are 15 words, from which you can choose the correct answer to each of the 15 questions.

When doing this exercise, break up each of the words you select into its component parts, trying to establish its meaning from its structure. To help you with this, have a dictionary at hand.

When you have filled in each of the 15 blank spaces with the letter of the word you think is correct, check your answers on page 218.

Vocabulary 1 (a)

(a) polyglot (b) amphibian (c) disenchantment (d) centipede (e) biped
(f) confluent (g) illiterate (h) antipathetic (i) retroactive (j) contravene
(k) tertiary (l) arch-enemy (m) paragon (n) triumvirate (o) impregnation

1 The most important and most dangerous of one's opponents is one's
___*l*___

2 A ___*e*___ is a two-footed animal.

3 A person or thing beyond comparison, a model of excellence, is known as a ___*m*___

4 Streams that flow together are said to be ___*f*___

5 A coalition of three men for the purposes of government or administration is called a ___*n*___

6 Many people in the world are not able to read; they are ___*g*___

7 ___*o*___ is the introduction of one substance into another.

8 Because people estimated that this creature had 100 legs, they called it a ___*d*___

9 ___*k*___ means third in rank, order or succession.

10 One opposite of fascination is _____

11 To go against restrictions laid down is to _____ the rules.

12 A creature that can live in both air and water is called an _____

13 _____ means operating in a backward direction.

14 A _____ is a person who speaks many languages.

15 If you have a strong feeling against something you are said to be

_____

Vocabulary 1 (b)

**(a) intravenous (b) autobiographer (c) abdicates (d) decalogue (e) atheist
(f) undermine (g) supercilious (h) isotherm (i) monomaniac (j) octagon (k)
catacomb (l) obfuscate (m) periscope (n) prominent (o) heminaopsia**

1 Someone who does not believe in God is an _____

2 He was a _____ because he had a fixation on a single object.

3 The Ten Commandments are often called the _____

4 An outstanding object or person is said to be _____

5 A plane figure with eight sides and angles is known as an _____

6 To _____ means to dig away the foundations, to bring down from
below.

7 A _____ is a graveyard below ground.

8 A person who _____ gives up a claim, resigns, gets away from a
situation.

9 An injection into the returning bloodstream is called an _____
injection.

10 When something gets in the way of light or meaning, it is said to

_____

11 To consider oneself to be above others is to possess a _____
attitude.

12 The medical condition in which one loses one half of one's field of
vision is known as _____

13 A _____ is an instrument that enables observers to look over an object.

14 A line on a map that connects those places having equal average temperature is called an _____

15 An _____ is a person who writes their own life story.

Vocabulary 1 (c)

(a) metaphysical (b) regurgitate (c) forebear (d) extravagate
(e) misconstrue (f) primordial (g) circumspect (h) diaphragm
(i) subjugate (j) predeterminable (k) nonentity (l) pentameter
(m) beneficence (n) pervade (o) malediction

1 A dividing membrane between two areas is called a _____

2 _____ applies to what is immaterial, incorporeal, super-sensory, beyond the physical.

3 A _____ is a curse.

4 _____ means to bring up or throw back from a deep place; to vomit.

5 A _____ is someone who is of no importance.

6 An ancestor may also be called a _____

7 When something passes through, permeates, extends and is diffused, it is said to _____

8 If you _____ you are going beyond ordinary limits.

9 A verse containing five feet is called a _____

10 _____ is charity, kindness or generosity.

11 If you are prudent and wary, and look all around before doing anything, you are _____

12 Something capable of being calculated beforehand is _____

13 That which has existed from the beginning, we call _____

14 To _____ means to subdue by superior force; to bring under the yoke.

15 If we interpret something wrongly, we _____

Detecting prefix

With your new knowledge of prefixes, read through any part of *The Speed Reading Book* that you have already completed and underline all the prefixes you can. You will find that they pop up at least once in almost every 100 words you read. Repeat this same exercise at the end of the next two sections, adding first suffixes and finally roots, especially concentrating on the 14 key power words.

Suffixes – getting to the point

You are now ready to learn the suffixes – letters, syllables and words placed at the end of words. As in the section on prefixes you will notice that most suffixes are taken from Latin and Greek.

The power of suffixes

This chapter introduces you to 51 suffixes, many of which are concerned with characteristics or qualities, or changing one part of speech into another (e.g. adjectives into adverbs).

51 suffixes

Suffix	Meaning	Example
-able, -ible (L)	capable of, fit for	durable, comprehensible
-acy (L, G)	state or quality of	accuracy
-age (L)	action or state of	breakage
-al, -ial (L)	relating to	abdominal
-an (-ane, -ian) (L)	the nature of	Grecian, African
-ance, -ence	quality or action of	insurance, corpulence
-ant (L)	forming adjectives of quality, nouns signifying a personal agent or something producing an effect	defiant, servant

-arium, -orium (L)	place for	aquarium, auditorium
-ary (L)	place for, dealing with	seminary, dictionary
-atable (L)	(see *-able*, *-ible*)	
-ate (L)	cause to be, office of	animate, magistrate
-ation, -ition (L)	action or state of	condition, dilapidation
-cle, -icle (L)	diminutive	icicle
-dom (E)	condition or control	kingdom
-en (E)	small	mitten
-en (E)	quality	golden, broken
-er (E)	belonging to	farmer, New Yorker
-ess (E)	feminine suffix	hostess, waitress
-et, -ette (L)	small	puppet, marionette
-ferous (L)	producing	coniferous
-ful (E)	full of	colourful, beautiful
-fy, -ify (L)	make	satisfy, fortify
-hood (E)	state or condition of	boyhood, childhood
-ia (L)	names of classes, names of places	bacteria, Liberia
-ian (L)	practitioners or inhabitants	musician, Parisian
-ic (G)	relating to	historic
-id(e) (L)	a quality	acid
-ine (G, L)	a compound	chlorine
-ion (L)	condition or action of	persuasion
-ish (E)	a similarity or relationship	childish, greenish
-ism (G)	quality or doctrine of	realism, socialism
-ist (G)	one who practises	chemist, pessimist
-itis (L)	inflammation of (medical)	bronchitis
-ity, -ety, -ty (L)	state or quality of	loyalty

Suffix	Meaning	Example
-ive (L)	nature of	creative, receptive
-ize, -ise (G)	make, practise, act like	modernize, advertise
-lent (L)	fullness	violent
-less (E)	lacking	fearless, faceless
-logy (G)	indicating a branch of knowledge	biology, psychology
-ly (E)	having the quality of	softly, quickly
-ment (L)	act or condition of	resentment
-metry, -meter (G)	measurement	gasometer, geometry
-mony	resulting condition	testimony
-oid (G)	resembling	ovoid
-or (L)	a state or action, a person who or thing which	error, governor, victor, generator
-osis	process or condition of	metamorphosis
-ous, -ose (L)	full of	murderous, anxious, officious, morose
-some	like	gladsome
-tude (L)	quality or degree of	altitude, gratitude
-ward (E)	direction	backward, outward
-y (E)	condition	difficulty

E = English, F = French, G = Greek, L = Latin.

Vocabulary mastermind

Vocabulary 2 (a)

(a) indefatigable (b) vignette (c) demobilise (d) epididymitis
(e) practitioner (f) ignominy (g) supremacy (h) platitude (i) untoward
(j) cursive (k) chauvinist (l) prioress (m) hedonism (n) embolden
(o) bondage

1 _____ is the condition of being marked with disgrace.

2 A _____ is a woman who governs a nunnery.

3 Someone who has very strong nationalistic feelings and who makes a practice of this somewhat exaggerated patriotism is called a _____

4 That which is intractable, unruly, perverse, which goes in the wrong unpredictable direction is _____

5 A _____ is one who works in a certain field, such as medicine.

6 A _____ is a comment or statement that is insipid and trite.

7 The unpleasant medical condition in which part of the testicle becomes irritated and inflamed is known as _____

8 To _____ is to imbue with the added qualities of courage, inspiration and fearlessness.

9 The doctrine of pursuing pleasure as the highest good is known as _____

10 If you are capable of working 12 hours a day without a rest, if you can engage in physical exercise for hours without seeming to get tired, then you are _____

11 Handwriting that is in the nature of a running hand, that forms the character rapidly without raising the pen, is known as _____ handwriting.

12 _____ is a small ornamental design, drawing or picture.

13 The quality or state of being uppermost, of having complete authority or power, is the state of _____

14 To _____ is to render something unable to operate or move; to disband.

15 _____ is the state of being bound or tied to something, either physically or mentally.

Vocabulary 2 (b)

(a) winsome (b) minimal (c) irritant (d) enervation (e) vociferous
(f) bellicose (g) aviary (h) corpuscle (i) magnate (j) hoydenish (k) baleful
(i) placid (m) osmosis (n) planetarium (o) martyrdom

1 Someone who places himself in a condition of suffering for his beliefs is placing himself in a position of _____

2 A diminutive particle of matter is sometimes known as a _____, although this term now usually applies to the small particles constituting blood.

3 A girl who is joyful, attractive and engaging is _____

4 A charge for something that relates to the lowest or smallest price is

_____

5 _____ is the process in which fluids tend to mix, even through porous membranes.

6 A _____ is a place where one goes to see models or projections of the solar system and other parts of the universe.

7 People who speak loudly and often are _____

8 _____ is the state of being exhausted.

9 A rude girl or tomboy is said to be _____

10 A _____ person is full of antagonism and the desire to quarrel or fight.

11 A place where birds are kept is known as an _____

12 A _____ look is one full of mischief or malice.

13 A _____ is a person who holds high rank or status.

14 To be gentle, quiet, peaceful and serene is to be _____

15 An _____ is that which provokes or produces discomfort or inflammation.

Vocabulary 2 (c)

(a) mundane (b) narcissistically (d) intelligentsia (d) insatiable (e) intensify
(f) rhetorician (g) deity (h) psychology (i) physiology (j) pestilence
(k) hardihood (l) annulment (m) anthropoid (n) metabolism (o) indolent

1 To be filled with the desire to do nothing, to be lazy, phlegmatic and idle is to be _____

2 A _____ is an eloquent speaker or writer.

3 The _____ is that class of educated people who tend to form much of public opinion.

4 _____ relates or pertains to the constant chemical changes in living matter.

5 An _____ is any creature that resembles man.

6 The branch of knowledge that deals with the body's organs and their functions is _____

7 A word for a state of boldness, courage and robustness is _____

8 That which is 'of the nature of the world' is often said to be _____

9 A disease, the qualities of which are plague-like and virulent, is often called a _____

10 _____ is the act of having a contract or marriage abolished.

11 To look at oneself _____ is to have the quality of the vain god who fell in love with his reflected image.

12 To _____ is to raise to a higher or more extreme degree.

13 When we attribute divine qualities to someone or something, we make them or it a _____

14 Someone whose appetite cannot be satisfied is _____

15 The branch of knowledge that deals with the human mind and its functioning is _____

Now check your answers on page 219.

Suffix expansion

After completing the vocabulary tests to your satisfaction, browse through a good dictionary, studying the various ways in which these suffixes are used. Keep a record of exceptionally good examples or examples that you find interesting and useful.

Now that you have learnt the beginnings and endings of modern English words, you can move on to roots, those elements from Latin and Greek that can be found anywhere in a modern word.

Roots – the key elements of words

The final vocabulary section deals with Latin and Greek roots – words from which others are derived – and also suggests five steps for continuing your vocabulary development.

Five steps to continue masterminding your vocabulary

1 Perform the exercise described in the previous section – browse through a good dictionary, studying the various ways in which the prefixes, suffixes and roots you have learnt are used. Keep a record of noteworthy examples and useful words.

2 Make a continuing and concentrated effort to introduce into your vocabulary at least one new word a day. New words are retained only if they are repeated a number of times, so once you have selected your word or words, make sure you use them often and effectively.

3 Be on the look-out for new and exciting words in conversations. If you are embarrassed about asking a speaker to define their terminology, make a quick mental note or jot down the word and look it up later.

4 Keep an eagle eye out for unfamiliar words in anything you read. Don't write them down as you read, but make a mark with a pencil and look them up afterwards.

5 If you feel so inclined, go to your local bookshop or library and ask for a book on vocabulary training – there are a number and most of them are quite helpful.

49 roots

Root	Meaning	Example
aer	air	aerate, aeroplane
am (from *amare*)	love	amorous, amateur, amiable
ann (from *annus*)	year	annual, anniversary
aud (from *audire*)	hear	auditorium, audit
bio	life	biography
cap (from *capire*)	take	captive
cap (from *caput*)	head	capital, per capita, decapitate
chron	time	chronology, chronic
cor	heart	cordial
corp	body	corporation
de	god	deify, deity
dic, *dict*	say, speak	dictate
duc (from *ducere*)	lead	aqueduct, duke, ductile
ego	I	egotism
equi	equal	equidistant
fac, *fic* (from *facere*)	make, do	manufacture, efficient
frat (from *frater*)	brother	fraternity
geo	earth	geology
graph	write	calligraphy, graphology, telegraph
loc (from *locus*)	place	location, local
loqu, *loc* (from *loqui*)	speak	eloquence, circumlocution
luc (from *lux*)	light	elucidate
man (from *manus*)	hand	manuscript, manipulate

Root	Meaning	Example
mit, *miss* (from *mittere*)	send	admit, permission
mort (from *mors*)	death	immortal
omni	all	omnipotent, omnibus
pat (from *pater*)	father	paternal
path	suffering, feeling	sympathy, pathology
ped (from *pes*)	foot	impede, millepede, pedal
phobia, *phobe*	fear	hydrophobe, xenophobia
photo	light	photography
pneum	air, breath, spirit	pneumonia
pos, *posit*	place	deposit, position
pot, *poss*, *poten* (from *ponere*)	be able	potential, possible
quaerere	ask, question, seek	inquiry, query
rog (from *rogare*)	ask	interrogate
scrib, *scrip* (from *scribere*)	write	scribble, script, inscribe
sent, *sens* (from *sentire*)	feel	sensitive, sentient
sol	alone	soloist, isolate
soph	wise	philosopher
spect (from *spicere*)	look	introspective, inspect
spir (from *spirare*)	breathe	inspiration
ten (from *tendere*)	stretch	extend, tense
ten (from *tenere*)	hold	tenant
therm (from *thermos*)	warm	thermometer
utilis	useful	utility, utilise
ven, *vent* (from *venire*)	come, arrive	advent, convenient
vert, *vers* (from *vertere*)	turn	revert, adverse
vid, *vis* (from *videre*)	see	supervisor, vision, provident

Vocabulary mastermind

Vocabulary 3 (a)

(a) expire (b) translucent (c) audition (d) sophist (e) annuity
(f) agoraphobia (g) querulous (h) amiable (i) thermal (j) dislocated
(k) graphology (l) impotent (m) telepathy (n) soliloquy (o) homologous

1 A person who is friendly and loveable is often described as _____

2 A _____ is a wise or would-be learned person.

3 Material through which light can travel is _____

4 You are _____ if you are unable to perform or act.

5 An _____ is a payment made yearly.

6 When an actor stands alone on a stage and speaks to himself, his speech is known as a _____

7 The word _____, which now usually means to pass away or die, derives from the idea of breathing out.

8 If a bone is out of joint, or misplaced, we say it is _____

9 The transference of thoughts from one mind to another over a distance is known as _____

10 _____ means to be alike in proportion, value or structure; to be in a corresponding position.

11 A person who is quarrelsome and discontented, and who complains in a questioning manner, is _____

12 _____ means pertaining to heat.

13 A trial hearing of an applicant for employment, especially in the case of actors and singers, is known as an _____

14 _____ is the controversial art of analysing personality from handwriting.

15 If you have a fear of open spaces, you suffer from _____

▶

Vocabulary 3 (b)

(a) tendentious (c) artefact (c) convene (d) decapitate (e) corporeal
(f) manciple (g) equinox (h) captivate (i) abduction (j) egocentric
(k) geomorphology (l) omniscient (m) interdict (n) utilitarian (o) patricide

1 If you behead someone you _____ them.

2 A _____ argument is one that stretches the truth in order to convince.

3 _____ is the study of the physical features of the crust of the Earth.

4 _____ is to take complete control of the attention; to overcome by charm of manner and appearance.

5 A person who considers themselves to be the centre of the universe is described as _____

6 _____, a term usually reserved for God, is occasionally applied to people who seem to know everything.

7 A _____ is someone who holds that actions are right only if they are useful.

8 An _____ is a statement that comes between a person and their intended action; a prohibition.

9 The murder of one's own father is known as _____

10 If something is made by, or results from art, if it is in some way artificial, we say it is an _____

11 The _____ is that time of year when both day and night are of equal length.

12 A _____ is a steward or servant (someone who waits on you hand and foot).

13 _____ means to cause to come together, to call to an assembly.

14 That which has a material body is said to be _____

15 _____ is leading or carrying away, usually by fraud or force.

Vocabulary 3 (c)

(a) chronometer (b) imposition (c) subrogation (d) elucidate (e) insensate
(f) desolation (g) morbid (h) vertigo (i) remittance (j) fraternise
(k) empathy (l) pneumatic (m) bioplasm (n) aerodynamics (o) tenacious

1 A person who is destitute of sense or given to extremes, we call

   _____

2 _____ is the power to project one's feelings into an object or
   person, and so reach full understanding.

3 _____ means to shed light on, to make clear.

4 A _____ drill is one that uses compressed air.

5 An instrument that finely measures time is a _____

6 A _____ person is one who holds on, no matter what the
   circumstances.

7 A _____ is money sent to you.

8 The science that deals with the forces exerted by air and by gaseous
   fluids is _____

9 The germinal matter for all living things is _____

10 When people associate as brothers, we say they _____

11 If something is _____, it reminds us of death.

12 An _____ may be defined as the act of placing or putting on; a
   burden, often unwelcome.

13 _____ is when you substitute someone else for yourself in
   respect of your legal rights.

14 .... refers to that which is deserted, laid waste, solitary,
   forsaken.

15 .... is a feeling of giddiness.

Now check your answers on pages 220–1.

With your increasing facility at speed reading and assimilating information, and your new-found ability to select and order information from newspapers and magazines and via your computer, laptop or PDA, it is just as essential to develop your speed reading skills in fictional works – in literature and poetry. We will discuss this in the next chapter.

Speed and range reading for literature and poetry

Why read poetry and literature? Because the great minds of history have left us, in them, easy stepping stones into the worlds of imagination, fantasy, ideas, philosophy, laughter and adventure; because by reading them you add to your own knowledge and your own historical and cultural data banks; because they are food for your soul. Literature is among the greatest expressions of human creativity. In this chapter you will be given the basic tools to appreciate it in the true sense of the word.

A novel is a massive conceptual achievement, and to appreciate it fully you need to be aware of the following aspects: plot, theme, philosophy, standpoint, character development, mood and atmosphere, setting, imagery, symbolism and use of language. Likewise, to appreciate poetry you should be aware of the different levels of meaning within any poem.

The more you understand each of these elements, the more your reading speed and comprehension will increase. If you are studying literature at school or university, the following aspects are invaluable as guide-posts for analysis. These guide-post areas provide good headings in essays and examinations – and make ideal main branches for Mind Map notes.

Many people proclaim that you cannot speed read a novel, because if you do you will lose the meaning and miss the rhythm of the language.

Nothing could be further from the truth.

A novel can be likened to an ocean. The little waves we see lapping the shore are in fact carried on waves that are nine ordinary waves long. These waves are themselves carried by waves that carry nine of them, and these larger waves are similarly carried by waves that carry nine of them. Some waves in the ocean are miles long.

It is similar with a novel. The rhythms of language can be likened to the surface waves. The other, larger rhythms are the other, deeper elements of the novel. The speed reader can appreciate them all.

The elements of literature

Plot

Plot is the basic structure of events in a novel – the storyline, if you wish. It may play a relatively minor role in primarily descriptive writing or a major role in the better whodunnits and mystery novels.

Theme

The theme is what the plot is about. For example, in *The Forsyte Saga*, a series of novels dealing with the history of a Victorian family, the main theme might variously be considered to be capitalism versus creativity, conservatism versus liberalism, conformity versus individuality, or wealth versus poverty. Sub-themes running parallel to the main one frequently occur in novels. Sub-themes often concern minor love affairs and secondary characters.

Philosophy

Philosophy is the system of ideas governing the universe of the work and can often be thought of as the author's commentary on the themes with which the book deals. Novelists known for the philosophical content in their novels include Dostoevsky, Dickens, Sartre and Thomas Mann.

Standpoint

Standpoint is not necessarily only the author's point of view or personal feeling about what he or she is writing. It is more often the physical standpoint from which the events described are seen. The author may, for instance, be all-knowing, standing apart, and viewing the past, present and future of the event he or she is describing (Henry James advocated abandoning this device, as he felt it clouded true representation). In contrast to this omniscient point of view, the author may place themselves in the first person (the author becomes the 'I' of the book), as in Hammond Innes' adventure stories and *Lolita* by Nabokov.

Character development

Character development concerns the changes the people in the story undergo. It may range from one extreme, such as Ian Fleming's James Bond, who remains completely unchanged throughout his series of novels, to Etienne in Zola's *Germinal*, who starts as a rebellious youth but evolves into a mature and dedicated man. Character development can also refer to the way the author presents the character, by description of their physical or mental character, movement, and so on.

Mood and atmosphere

These two terms refer to the manner in which the author evokes a sense of reality or unreality and the emotional response of the reader. Some people prefer to use only one of these terms, although they can be distinguished from each other: mood can be described as the reaction felt by the individual to the atmosphere of a piece of writing. For example, the atmosphere in Edgar Allan Poe's stories might be described as morbid and menacing, while the mood of his readers might vary from frightened to exhilarated.

Setting

Setting refers to the physical locale and the time period in which the events take place. Because the setting is usually quite apparent, its importance is often underestimated – and yet the slightest variations in time and place often have very significant effects on plot, mood, atmosphere and imagery.

Imagery

Imagery is often described as the use of simile and metaphor, meaning that objects, people and events are described in creative or fanciful language. The root word 'image' is perhaps most useful in coming to an understanding of this term. For example, Sir Walter Scott, in *The Heart of Midlothian*, described Edinburgh as 'the pulsating heart core of the Scottish scene'; and Dickens, in *A Tale of Two Cities*, when describing the uncovering of a prisoner buried alive for 18 years, uses images of death and burial – heavy wreaths, cadaverous colours and emaciated heads and figures. Darkness and shadows prevail.

Symbolism

Simply explained, symbolism means that one thing stands for or represents another. Throughout much of literary history, the Earth, for example, has symbolised fertility and reproduction. Since the publication of Freud's theories, symbolism has become an increasingly important element in literature, with a new emphasis on the sexual. Any jutting object, such as a gun or tree, may be used to symbolise the male sex organ; and any circular or hollow object, such as a box or a circular pond, can be used to symbolise the female sex organ.

An excellent example of symbolism can be found in *A Tale of Two Cities*, when a cask of red wine is spilt. The populace drinks the muddy dregs with relish, signifying the desperate hunger that later results in the spilling of real blood in the French Revolution. In D. H. Lawrence's *The Fox*, the frozen waste in which two women live symbolises their frigidity, while the male character's shooting of a fox (symbolising the general male 'threat') places him in the dominant male role. Symbolism is often a great deal more obscure than in these examples, and the reader who understands it may be one of the very few who grasps the full meaning of much of great literature.

Use of language

Authors' use of language varies from the tough masculine style of Hemingway to the flowing and poetic prose of Nabokov. The language that an author uses is always revealing, and if you pay careful attention to it you will often gain far deeper insight into the shades of meaning and mood within the work.

In discussing these aspects of the novel, I have dealt with each item separately, but it is important to remember they are all inextricably linked. The very setting of a story, for example, may be symbolic – and so it is with the other aspects. When you read literature, always try to be aware of the intricate interrelationships between all these aspects.

EXERCISE

Novel

Choose a novel by one of your favourite authors and read it, using all the speed reading skills you have acquired so far. Make sure you preview it, Mind Map it, use your guide throughout, and analyse it according to the elements of the novel.

Poetry

Many people insist that poetry should be read very slowly. Our talking speed is about 200 wpm, but many of us tend to read poetry at less than 100 wpm. Actually this hinders a proper appreciation, for a slow, plodding trudge through a poem effectively destroys the natural rhythm and consequently conceals much of the meaning from the reader. In schools, this problem is made worse by teachers who fail to correct students when they read each line as though the meaning lay at the end. This is often simply not the case. Sophisticated poets let their meaning flow through the lines.

The best approach to reading poetry is as follows:

1 Begin with a very rapid preview, enabling you to find out roughly what the poem is about and where it leads.

2 Do a rapid but more thorough reading to get a more accurate idea of the way the lines relate to each other and the way the thought and rhythm interlink and progress.

3 Take a leisurely ramble through the poem, concentrating on areas of particular interest.

4 Read the poem aloud.

In the final analysis, speed is often not a main final goal when it comes to literature and poetry – which can best be likened to listening to music or appreciating art. One does not listen to Beethoven's Fifth Symphony once and throw out the recording with the triumphant claim, 'Well, I've done that at an average speed of 33 rpm!'

When reading literature and poetry, bring to bear on it all your knowledge and personal judgement, and if you feel it is the kind of writing you wish to treasure forever, forget about speeding through it and reserve it for those occasions when time is not so pressing.

Buy or borrow a book of poems, and read in the way described. Your approach should be to apply whatever seems most appropriate from all that you have learnt. You should now begin to make your own decisions about the way you will tackle any given material.

When making these decisions, there are certain things that should remain constant, including your use of a guide, your focus on the goals for the reading, and your continuing ability to accelerate your reading speed while maintaining and improving your comprehension.

Poetry

Read the following poems by the author, using the formula outlined earlier. A clue to the first one is that it relates very strongly to the information in Chapter 4. A clue to the second is that it relates to the ongoing theme of speed reading: the eye/brain perceptual system. The author would appreciate your interpretations and comments.

Dumbfounded

A Picture is Worth a Thousand Words.
I am led to understand that my three hundred million
retinal light-receivers absorb
one thousand two hundred million photons
each
one five-hundredth of a second

Five hundred
reality
snapshots of You,
every second

As I gaze,
amazed,

and you ask somewhere in the far distance:

'What do you think?'

'Why don't you talk to me?'

Cliff and Man

The cliff-edge beckoned
asked him to walk near,
dared him to stand on edge;

but he tricked Her,
approached on cat feet

and buckled
his own length away –
slid his body forward;
safely moved his Seeing
over.

And she, laughing, made him swim,
stretched him in Her space,
dragged his mind's laceworks
down to the rock-mossed edges of depth,
reeled him down Her sides and ledges,
yo yo'd his Eye
and down and distantly
roared at him with Her sea.

He wrestled with her offering,
warped his tiny space;
engulfed Her.

So she flung him Her earth-bird
sea gull
who wrung his mind
to ecstasy,
rode the funnel
of Her deepness
feathered the winds that shoved him
still on that cliff edge
swept any curve
stilled any wind-rush
dropped in any air rise
erased ledge and edgeness for him
drew him   drew him out

The engulfer
Engulfed.

Now you have learnt how speed reading can help you to appreciate literature and poetry fully, let's try another self-test. This one will give you further information on your amazing brain. While reading it, bring to bear all the relevant knowledge you have gained from *The*

Speed Reading Book, and do everything you can to surpass your previous performances. Your continuing success in all fields of speed reading depends on your personal decision to continue the course you have begun, and on the capacity of your brain to read, assimilate, comprehend, recall, communicate and create – a capacity which we know approaches the infinite!

SELF-TEST 6

Your brain – the enchanted loom, by Tony Buzan
The human brain and its potential

'The human brain is an enchanted loom where millions of flashing shuttles weave a dissolving pattern, always a meaningful pattern, though never an abiding one. It is as if the Milky Way entered upon some cosmic dance.'

Sir Charles Sherrington

To compare the brain with a galaxy is in fact a modest analogy. Every intact person on our planet carries around his three-and-a-half-pound mass of tissue without giving much thought to it; yet every normal brain is capable of making more patterned interconnections than there are atoms in the universe.

The brain is composed of about ten billion nerve cells and each one is capable of being involved in a vast series of complex connections thousands of times every second. At a mathematical level alone, the complexity is astounding. There are ten billion neurons in the brain and each one has a potential of connections of 1028. In more comprehensible terms, this means that, if the theoretical number of potential connections in your brain were to be written out, you would get a figure beginning with 1, followed by about ten and a half million kilometres of noughts.

All this is potential, of course, and, despite the manifold detailed discoveries of neuro-physiology, it is your brain's potential which is most exciting. It is undisputed that we all under-use our brains – if we do not actually abuse them. This is hardly surprising. Few of us will ever see a human brain. Those who have, do not describe it as a particularly remarkable sight.

It is understandable that a concert pianist or a carpenter should value his hands above all, that a painter should cherish his eyes, that a runner should be most concerned about his legs. But hands are as useless without a brain as the piano itself without a player. The brain's potential has been largely

▶

underestimated precisely because of its omnipresence. It is involved in all we do, in everything that happens to us, and so we note that which is different in each experience, overlooking that without which nothing is possible for us.

We have been too much concerned with differences rather than potential in another, more important, sense. Since we have known that such things as brains existed, we have devoted most of our efforts not to improving them but to devising systems to demonstrate the differences between them. This applies not only in education, where pass or fail is the ultimate criterion, but in every aspect of our lives. We are American or Chinese, scholar or peasant, artist or scientist. These distinctions exist, of course, and it would be foolish to dismiss them completely. But the inherent ability of each brain in its own right is important too. In every head is a formidable powerhouse, a compact, efficient organ whose capacity seems to expand further towards infinity the more we learn of it.

John Rader Platt expressed this view:

> If this property of complexity could somehow be transformed into visible brightness so that it would stand forth more clearly to our senses, the biological world would become a walking field of light compared to the physical world. The sun with its great eruptions would fade to a pale simplicity compared to a rose bush, an earth worm would be a beacon, a dog would be a city of light, and human beings would stand out like blazing suns of complexity, flashing bursts of meaning to each other through the dull night of the physical world between. We would hurt each other's eyes. Look at the haloed heads of your rare and complex companions. Is it not so?

The basis of this 'property of complexity' is the nerve cell – the neuron. Even those which are microscopically small are in themselves remarkably complex. Neurons differ from most other cells in that they are a more complicated shape and have many branching prolongations which can connect with each other to transmit nerve impulses. Throughout the nervous system the neurons vary tremendously in size. Some, running from the toes or the fingers into the spinal cord, can be as much as a metre in length. Others, in the cerebral cortex for example, are more than a thousand times smaller.

Everything we do, from moving a muscle to thinking great thoughts, involves intricate neuronal functioning. Whatever the activity, however, the process is similar and is founded on the excitation of the neuron. The process consists of electrochemical signals being passed from one neuron to another: not just singly or slowly but in rapid, multiple waves of communication. Each neuron has a main body which contains specific chemical and genetic information, and an axon which conducts the vital nerve impulses. It will also have a variable number of branching dendrites. These are the receivers of the impulses or information, either directly from a sense organ or, more commonly, from other neurons in the tapestry of connections.

The precise location of the transmission of the impulse from one neuron to another is your synapse where the information 'flows' across a microscopic gap not unlike the spark plug gap or the distributor points in the internal combustion engine. The physics and chemistry of this process are immensely intricate. In the synapse chemical substances are released which enable the electrical impulses to be transmitted and the synapse has a threshold which affects how readily the impulse is accepted. In familiar or reflex activity the threshold is lower so that the circuit operates more readily. A higher threshold means that the signal is more difficult to transmit.

An impulse from a single neuron causes activation in the synapses it forms with others and even the simplest mental or physical process involves certainly hundreds of neurons receiving and transmitting impulses in complex cascading waves of communication and co-operation. A hundred thousand neuronal 'messages' a second is commonplace.

Everything we do and experience, therefore, involves this intricate bio-electrical process – from playing tennis to paying the bills. This is not as perplexing as it might seem. We know that the eyes do not in themselves see: they are merely lenses. The ears do not in themselves hear: they are, so to speak, microphones. When we watch a cricket match on television we do not see the players themselves but electronic representations of them on the picture tube. What is between the cat you see in the flesh and your brain's image of the cat is a series of neuro-physiological processes, just as there is a series of electronic processes between the actual cricket match and the image you see on television.

Our brains are, almost literally, everything. We can give more to them and in turn, and in addition, they can give to us. The brain is our secret, silent weapon. If we can just begin to use more of its power, we will indeed see a light that will hurt, but astonish, our eyes. To quote John Rader Platt again:

Many of our most sensitive spirits today still see Man as the antihero; the helpless victim of weapons and wars, of governments and mechanisms and soul-destroying organisations and computers – as indeed he is. But in the midst of this man-made and inhuman entropy, like a Fourth Law of Man, there grows up even in the laboratories, a realisation that Man is also mysterious and elusive, self-determining and perpetual. A lighthouse of complexity and the organising child of the universe. One equipped and provided for to stand and choose and act and control and be.

STOP YOUR TIMER NOW!

Length of time: _____ min

Next, calculate your reading speed in words per minute (wpm) by dividing the number of words in the passage (in this case, 1250) by the time (in minutes) you took.

$$\text{Words per minute (wpm)} = \frac{\text{number of words}}{\text{time}}$$

When you have completed your calculation, enter the number in the wpm slot at the end of this paragraph and also enter it on your progress graph and chart on pages 222–3.

Words per minute: _____

Self-test 6: Comprehension

1　Who described the human brain as an enchanted loom?
　(a)　Sir Charles Sherrington
　(b)　Peter Russell
　(c)　John Rader Platt
　(d)　Isaac Newton
2　The human brain weighs approximately:
　(a)　2½ lb
　(b)　2 lb
　(c)　3½ lb
　(d)　3 lb
3　The number of potential connections for one brain cell is:
　(a)　1010
　(b)　1019
　(c)　1028

(d) 10

4 Since we have known that such things as brains existed, we have devoted most of our efforts:
(a) to improving them
(b) to devising systems to demonstrate the differences between them
(c) to dismissing them
(d) to destroying them

5 Who compared the complexity of the brain, transformed into visible brightness, with the physical world?
(a) Sir Charles Sherrington
(b) John Rader Platt
(c) Galileo
(d) Einstein

6 'The sun with its great eruptions would fade to a pale simplicity compared to a _____.'

7 And 'a dog would be a':
(a) rose bush
(b) beacon
(c) sun
(d) city of light

8 The basis of the 'property of complexity of the brain' is the:
(a) nerve cell or neuron
(b) dendrite
(c) axon
(d) cortex

9 Neurons differ from most other cells in that they are:
(a) simpler
(b) more complicated in shape
(c) bigger
(d) smaller

10 Neurons can reach:
(a) a centimetre
(b) an inch
(c) a foot
(d) a metre

11 The process of electrochemical signals being passed from one neuron
     to another progresses:
     (a) singly and slowly
     (b) in rapid, multiple waves of communication
     (c) faster than the speed of light
     (d) only when we are thinking
12 An axon:
     (a) is bigger than the brain cell
     (b) is the main part of the synapse
     (c) conducts vital nerve impulses
     (d) is another name for the brain cell
13 The physics and chemistry of the processes in the
     synapse are fundamentally simple.   *True/False*
14 A common number of neuronal 'messages' per second is:
     (a) 100
     (b) 1000
     (c) 10,000
     (d) 100,000
15 Who wrote about the Fourth Law of Man?
     (a) Einstein
     (b) Freud
     (c) Platt
     (d) Sherrington

Check your answers against those on page 217. Then divide your score by
15 and multiply by 100 to calculate your percentage comprehension.

Comprehension score: _____ out of 15

_____ per cent

Now enter your score on your progress graph and chart on pages 222–3.

Assimilating printed and online information

This chapter provides you with highly efficient new ways to extract relevant information from newspapers, magazines and computer screens, which, together, make up more than 50 per cent of most people's reading (in some cases, 100 per cent).

Newspapers, magazines, computer screens and PDA displays are some of your windows on the world and, increasingly, the universe. It is possible, by understanding their nature, and some new approaches to them, to increase your efficiency in this arena by a factor of ten.

Newspapers

Newspapers are so much a part of our everyday life that we seldom stop to think that they are a very recent development. Before the twentieth century, the voice of journalism was virtually non-existent as far as the masses were concerned. Newspapers were, in the main, news-sheets containing very little analysis or editorial comment. There was, however, one noteworthy exception, *The Times*, whose critical reports on the Crimean War in 1855 have been cited as influential in the downfall of the Cabinet and the reorganisation of the British army.

The nineteenth century saw a steady growth in the world press, stimulated by the introduction of the Foudrinier machine, which produced paper in a continuous sheet. Parallel to this development was the universal growth of communication networks and education: more information was required more rapidly, and more people were able to read. As a result, many of the world's newspapers were founded between 1840 and 1900.

In the early twentieth century, newspapers flourished, but even now, after a fairly short existence, many are entering more difficult times. Reasons cited include the rise of television with its moving-image coverage of news events, and the spread of the computer news bulletin and the Internet, which give more immediate and personal coverage of news events. Newspapers are currently fighting back, integrating themselves with online versions.

In the West we may well be entering a time in which the newspaper will change its function, dealing less with immediate news and more with summaries, analyses and comment.

Approaches to reading newspapers

Having viewed newspapers in their international and historical context, let us briefly discuss how best to read them:

1 First, it is most important to have an organised approach. Many people spend hours reading a newspaper and come away feeling no more enlightened than when they began.

2 Whatever newspaper you read, it is always helpful to decide beforehand exactly what your aim is. To assist you in this decision, always rapidly preview the newspaper before you read it, selecting the various passages and articles that you wish to read more thoroughly.

3 Make a note of the layout and typography. Knowing where articles are continued, for instance, saves a lot of page-turning and fumbling.

4 Most people have a tendency to buy a newspaper that supports their general views – in other words, they give themselves a little pat on the back every morning or evening. It can be a most interesting

exercise to buy a different newspaper each day for a week, comparing and contrasting the different layouts, the political bias, the approach of the reporters, the interpretation of news events and the extent of the coverage. Try this during the coming week.

5 Newspaper reports should be checked for accuracy. I am sure that those of you who have been involved in a function or event that was reported the next day have often thought 'That's nothing like what happened at all!' News is written by people who are likely to be biased or to be following a particular editorial policy. This 'misreporting', if we can call it that, is not necessarily intentional. Each person tends to see any given situation in a different light. Newspaper reporters are individuals, and they may be seeing a given event from a different physical location. For example, being in the middle of a stampeding crowd and being in a building watching that crowd stampede are bound to produce different reports.

6 Accepting this basic and inevitable bias, we move on to the reporting of the event itself. The journalist will take down brief notes of what he or she wishes to report, will spend time travelling back to their computer, and will then reconstruct in their mind's eye the events that have taken place. Once again, there will be slight and inevitable changes in emphasis, which will be embellished by the words used to describe the situation. Once the report has been written, it has to be edited, and then re-edited, before finally reaching the pages of the newspaper. It can be seen that, even with the most sincere of intentions, it is almost impossible to give a completely objective report. Newspapers, magazines and journals should therefore be read with a far more critical eye than they usually are, and what they report should be checked against other sources such as radio, television, other journals and computer networks.

7 Having assimilated steps 1–6, you can now take your reading of newspapers a giant leap forward by following these guidelines:

(a) Decide on your main goals in reading a newspaper, and endeavour to stick to these goals as closely as possible.

(b) Skim and scan articles and pages using the techniques outlined in Chapter 9

(c) Use a guide throughout.

(d) As you skim and scan, mark any articles that are of particular interest to you.

(e) Cut out any articles that are going to be of lasting use and interest to you.

(f) Throw the rest of the newspaper out as soon as possible.

(g) Use a Mind Map to record any major new information or any information that is building on a daily or weekly or annual basis.

Magazines

Magazines are like newspapers in most respects, and therefore the approaches outlined so far in this chapter will also apply to them. However, there are a number of significant differences that are worth noting:

● The articles in magazines tend to be longer than the articles in newspapers.

● Magazines tend to have more illustrations and more colour in those illustrations compared with newspapers.

● Magazines are not produced within such a tight schedule as newspapers, and therefore they tend to be more discursive.

Because of these differences, it is usually easier to pick out a logical structure in a magazine article. Indeed, most magazine journalists are taught that they should 'tell your reader what you're going to tell 'em, tell 'em, and then tell 'em you've told 'em.'

This means that most magazine articles start with a 'teaser' or 'grabber', immediately followed by a cogent statement of the purpose of the article. All this is the 'tell 'em what you're going to tell 'em'.

Next will follow the main body and bulk of the article. In a good article, this will include logical arguments, illustrations, photographs and other elements drawing on the cortical skills to help persuade you of the writer's point. This is the 'tell 'em'.

The final part of the article, its climax, is where the writer uses some sort of dramatic or 'punchy' ending, incorporating a review of the main thesis, in an attempt to ram home the point. This is the 'tell 'em you've told 'em'.

Knowing this structure will allow you to scan all magazine articles far more effectively, for you will know precisely where to look for the information. Skimming will also be much easier when you do it with this article structure uppermost in your mind.

Having a magazine blitz

One wonderful and enjoyable way of getting through your magazines is to have a monthly 'magazine blitz'. This means saving all your magazines for one special monthly occasion, in which you prepare yourself for a super meta-guide speed through every page of every magazine you have collected that month.

It is useful to set your metronome to at least 60 beats per minute and to force yourself to turn the page with every beat, whipping your meta-guide down the page. The purpose of this exercise is for you to select only those pages from the magazine that you feel may be of interest to you. You should immediately rip these pages out and continue progressing through the magazine at your metronome pace. The pages you select should include articles of particular interest, but they may also include photographs or images that are particularly appealing, cartoons you especially like, advertisements that may be of use, and so on. These you keep in a neat pile, discarding with a flourish the irrelevant material.

In the Buzan Centre Advanced Reading Courses, a fascinating statistic has emerged: in over 99 per cent of cases, the average amount of material retained after this first reading is between 2 per cent and 10 per cent. Some students feel so relieved by their sudden release from the massive weight of unread-material-that-had-to-be-completed that they whoop and holler gleefully as they fling their discarded magazines into the centre of the classroom.

Once you have selected the relevant material, do a second read-through, this time sorting and collating the pieces into appropriate categories. Because of the similarity of magazines aimed at the same readership, you will often find that a number of articles cover similar points; your reading volume is thus reduced even further. Particularly beautiful images or witty cartoons can either be interspersed in other reading material to give you delightful breaks as you study, or they can be filed in their own special sections.

Employing this approach usually results in less than 1 per cent of the magazine actually needing to be read – saving the other 99 per cent of effort.

Computer screens

Reading from a computer screen or PDA display can be made far easier by adjusting two main variables: the environment (especially lighting) and your reading technique.

Improving your computer environment

1 **Lighting** – experiment with different kinds of lighting. You need an even, clear, soft light, with no glare. Inappropriate lighting can reduce your reading speed by as much as 50 per cent, so make sure that yours is appropriate for your needs.

2 **Contrast** – high contrast makes reading easier and therefore comprehension better and speed faster. Different people prefer different colour combinations for print and background, so once again experiment to find the one most suitable for you. Common favourites include black print on a white background, orange on black, and navy-blue on white. Whatever your preference, adjust the contrast and brightness of your screen until you achieve the greatest possible print clarity. If the light in your office varies, vary your screen contrast to compensate.

Using speed reading techniques on your computer screen

Use a guided reading technique – that is, with a long thin guide, such as a chopstick or knitting needle. This is particularly useful when reading from a computer screen. It allows you to read more comfortably and at a greater distance from the screen. The technique is identical to reading from the page of a book.

1 You can use the guide in conjunction with the computer line pacer. Press the down arrow, setting it at an appropriate speed, and let the guide cruise backwards and forwards as the pages reveal themselves before you. If your posture and poise are

appropriate, you will be more relaxed and at ease than the person who does not use a guide.

2 Make sure that every 10 or 15 minutes of computer speed reading is punctuated by a visual rest in which you allow your eyes to wander around the room and, ideally, into the medium and long distance. In this way, you eliminate standard eye fatigue. Using this technique will get rid of the eye strain so commonly experienced by computer readers, and will help to eliminate a stiff neck, restricted breathing, hunched shoulders and lower back pain.

3 Choose the right typeface. The modern computer has a number of typefaces. Don't get stuck on a 'standard' one: select the typeface that, at the time, feels easiest for your eye/brain system to assimilate.

4 Choose the right line spacing. Your computer has a variety of line space settings. Choose the one that suits you best. Most popular is single-spaced setting, for this allows your peripheral vision a greater opportunity to take in large chunks of information per fixation.

Executive secretaries on a recent Management Centre Europe course for assistants to the directors of multinational organisations reported that 20–60 per cent of their day was spent reading information directly from computer screens or from print-outs. They said that, with the increase in the amount of material faxed and emailed, these percentages were steadily increasing. The need for speed reading is thus even greater in the modern office.

The computer speed reading approaches outlined above will at least triple your speed on the computer screen. This means that the number of hours you will need to spend in front of the screen will be considerably reduced, thus further easing the strain on your eyes.

The world of the web and internet has added a new dimension to reading and a new importance to the need and necessity of knowing *how* to read.

Reading on the web can be likened to reading a book in which you have the opportunity, on every page, to branch out or wander off or 'go with the flow' in limitless directions. The World Wide Web has become an indefinitely large, semi-chaotic, collection of information in a profusion of texts, graphics, images, soundbites and animations posted by anyone. This makes it essential that the online reader has the ability to discriminate between the little relevant and the vast irrelevant floods of data. There is also the vital requirement of storing the information selected.

With a full knowledge of how to read and speed read you can negotiate these 'currents' of information with confidence, ease, and success. Without such knowledge you will drift into backwaters, or worse into rapids, or even 'Niagaras' on every page.

In this new reading universe you *must* be able to take control; you *must* be able to select the right directions and navigate the currents while avoiding the rapids and 'Niagaras'.

Dr Cynthia Doss, who has been working with me in this field has identified, in her groundbreaking study on hypertext reading, three key types of hypertext reader, only one of whom you wish to be:

1 ***The Novice Reader*** is one who clicks on all or most of the hyperlinks in the hypertext. Novice online readers do not skim through the text in the hyperlink as they should; they read almost every 'unnecessary' line in the text in the hyperlink. At the end, the novice online reader loses focus on the reading purposes or leaves the hyperlink even more confused or disorientated. This is because the novice reader is unwittingly attempting to read the web in the same way they traditionally read a book. If they applied the speed reading elements of this book, they would become skilled hypertext readers who would be able to select, manage and comprehend frames of pages that could lead to information overload.

2 ***The Cautious Reader*** is the one who, afraid of being swamped by the tsunamis of information, either ignores all the hyperlinks or just clicks on the hyperlink only when he or she has finished reading the paragraph, page or the whole text. The cautious online reader does not engage actively in reading relevant hypertext content.

3 ***The Skilled Reader*** (the one you are becoming!) is the one who monitors his or her comprehension of, and goals for, the text *before* deciding whether or not to click on the hyperlink.
If the skilled online readers find that they have understood the paragraph or page they would not click on the hyperlink.

This is an effective strategy to avoid wasting time or getting distracted. However, if the skilled readers entered a hyperlink they would only scan and skim rapidly for only the relevant information.

In her work with Tony Buzan, Dr Cynthia Doss has confirmed that the skilled reader will be the one who applies all the main principles as outlined in the new definition of reading (see page 18) and the one who uses Mind Maps as the ultimate hypertext navigation tool. The Mind Map allows you to navigate hypertext – to gather, organize, evaluate and take action on a vast amount of sometimes random information, knowledge and ideas – like a master game-player (see *The Mind Map Book*). Mind mapping software (see **www.imindmap.com**) especially enables you to move topics and subtopics around, attach notes, links and documents to them that provide meaning and context, and play 'what if' with your ideas.

In conclusion, hypertext is no big deal: you simply require the same fundamental, marvellous, wonderful piece of equipment (your eye-brain system) you have been using for normal text reading. The words are the same, the sentences are the same, the printing is the same, the information is the same; the only difference is that your brain needs to jump from screen item to screen item and it needs to have a matrix, a manager of that information. Speed reading with the support of Mind Maps will help you manage and 'surf' hypertext successfully and rapidly.

At this point, you are approaching the tail end of the self-tests. Before completing Self-test 7, increase your motivation, practise acceleration exercises with your guide, make sure you are holding the book a good distance from you, and preview well as explained in Chapter 12, to help you increase your speed and comprehension even further. At this stage you should also consider my study skills techniques for study reading set out in *The Buzan Study Skills Handbook* and the use of Mind Maps to search your memory for previous knowledge of the topic (see *The Mind Map Book* and *The Memory Book*), thus ensuring you have an appropriate mind set. Before we tackle the penultimate test, here is a very brief recap of my study technique, broken down into preparation and application.

Study reading is an area to which all the techniques contained in this book can be applied. You can then add to that my BOST® (Buzan Organic Study Technique) study skills, which incorporate all the brain-compatible skills, including Mind Mapping, the memory principles and systems, and the speed reading processes. BOST is explained in full in *The Buzan Study Skills Handbook* but, very briefly, the technique is divided into two parts, preparation and application:

1 Preparation

    (a) *Browse* – use the previewing skills taught in Chapter 12 to gain a bird's eye view of the text.

    (b) *Time and amount* – set the time periods and the quantities of material to be covered in these periods (Figures 15.1 and 15.2).

    (c) *Previous knowledge Mind Map* – using a Mind Map, search your memory for previous knowledge on the topic, thus ensuring that you have an appropriate mental set.

    (d) *Goals and objectives* – establish clearly why you are reading the material and what you want to get out of it.

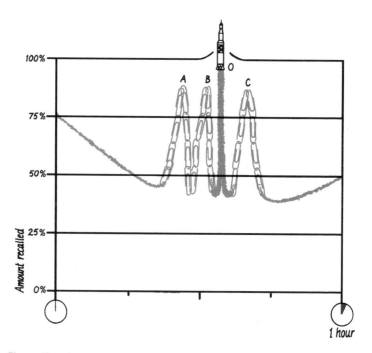

*Figure 15.1 **Graph showing that we recall more from the beginning and end of a learning period. We also recall more when things are associated or linked (A, B, C) and more when things are outstanding or unique (O).***

The Speed Reading Book

2 Application

(a) *Overview* – do a second, deeper browse, using your goals and questions to select appropriate foundation information.

(b) *Preview* – having established the basic structure of the information, begin to zoom in on the relevant parts, focusing on beginnings and endings (Figure 15.2).

(c) *Inview* – fill in the bulk of the remaining information and build up your Mind Map, leaving difficult areas for the final stage.

(d) *Review* – this is the final integration. Complete your Mind Map, solve any remaining problems, answer any remaining questions and complete all your goals.

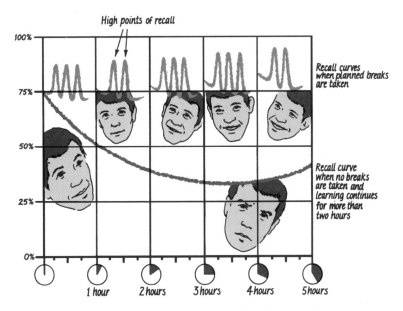

Figure 15.2 Recall during learning, with and without breaks. A learning period of 20–50 minutes produces the best relationship between understanding and recall.

Embrace creativity and watch your profits grow!,
by Tony Buzan

The best way to get a good idea is to get a lot of ideas!
Linus Pauling

Crisis + creativity = opportunity

Credit crunch, financial downturn, falling sales, rising prices, budget cuts – are you concerned about how these will hit your bottom line? Imagine if you could improve the brain power of each one of your managers and employees, especially your own. In a marketplace where competition is fierce and it is so difficult to maintain corporate flair and individuality, it really is possible to learn techniques that can affect your turnover in a positive way. By focusing on learning, and practising creative behaviours, you will energise both your core business and the individuals within it.

I have spent many years researching the workings of the brain and transforming this knowledge into models that can empower each person to use his/her intellect to the maximum. These form the central triptych of my training sessions: Mind Maps; Memory; and Speed Reading and Information Management. In essence they constitute a Creativity Toolkit for the Brain.

What is creativity and why should you work creatively?

Creativity is the development of original ideas, images and solutions based on existing old ideas by using Imagination and Association. We see here how important the current knowledge base is in promoting new concepts.

The driving force behind your creativity is your imagination. Creativity involves going on imaginative journeys, taking people into original and previously unexplored realms. These new associations give rise to the new realisations that the world calls 'creative breakthroughs'. Thus it becomes clear that memory is the use of imagination and association to hold the past in its appropriate place and to re-create the past in the present, whereas creativity is the use of imagination and association to plant the present thought in the future, and to re-create the present thought in some future time. Working creatively produces multiple ideas, which can then be fully assessed and analysed, with the very best of these innovations being processed and turned into products or services. This is where your company can reap the rewards of such creativity through creative behaviours, and the ensuing valuable intellectual property, which increases turnover and pushes up profits.

It is easy to call yourself 'creative' but actually becoming creative requires that you understand what creativity is, and learn how to develop that creativity. Dedication and energy are then needed to embed this new way of thinking into the culture of your business. It means really working at it and showing others how to do the same.

Becoming a truly creative organisation is not achieved easily. It requires a radical paradigm shift in thinking and action. Every brain in your company is an infinite resource that must be stimulated and developed to maintain your competitive edge in the marketplace. People often talk of the brain as being a 'Problem Solving Organ' when in fact it is a 'Solutions Finding Organ',

Once your employees understand that creativity is not something you have a go at once a week for an hour, they will understand that creativity is available to everyone – all the time.

Creativity can – and should – be applied in all areas of your business. Being creative can be difficult when you are obliged to work within codes of conduct and rules and regulations, which seem to deaden all levels of thinking. That is precisely when you need to look for fresh perspectives. This can feel dangerous at first, but it soon becomes exciting and liberating.

How can you achieve this? By applying techniques that, once they become second-nature, will support you in all your endeavours, whether you are in meetings, managing clients and projects, developing business etc.

Mind Maps and creativity

In a *Newsweek* article in 2006, entitled 'The Road Ahead: How "intelligent agents" and Mind Mappers are taking our information democracy to the next stage', Bill Gates stated his conviction that:

'... a new generation of Mind Mapping software can be used as a digital "blank slate" to help connect and synthesize ideas and data – and ultimately create new knowledge ... and mental models to help people mine and assess the value of all that information ...'

Mind Mapping is the intrinsic Mental Model, which lies at the heart of his statement. Why is a Mind Map such a powerful creative tool? Creating a Mind Map requires 'whole-brain', synergetic thinking that reflects the explosive nature of the neurons zapping across the brain in search of new connections during the process of thinking. It is like some vast pinball machine with billions of silver balls whizzing at the speed of light from flipper to flipper.

Your brain does not think linearly or sequentially like a computer. It thinks multi-laterally: radiantly. When you create a Mind Map the branches grow outwards to form another level of sub-branches encouraging you to create more ideas out of each thought you add to it – just as your brain does. Also, because all the ideas on the Mind Map are linked to each other, it helps your brain to make great leaps of understanding and imagination through association. Mind Maps are the thinking tool to unlock your brain power; they reflect the internal Mind Maps of your brain. If you have lost sight of your goals, or the bigger picture has become blurred, draw a Mind Map and the overview that emerges will bring clarity and potential to the forefront.

Quick start: Mind Mapping

Start in the centre with an image of the topic, using at least 3 colours.

Use images, symbols, codes and dimension throughout your Mind Map.

Select key words and print, using upper or lower case letters.

Only one word or image to sit on its own line.

The lines must be connected, starting from the central image. The central lines are thicker, organic and flowing, becoming thinner as they radiate our from the centre.

Make the lines the same length as the word or image.

Use colours – your own code – throughout the Mind Map.

Develop your own personal style of Mind Mapping.

Use emphasis and show associations in your Mind Map.

Keep the Mind Map clear by using hierarchy, numerical order or outlines to embrace your branches.

Memory and creativity

What's memory got to do with it? I have developed a new formula that demonstrates, for the first time, the intimate relationship between memory and creativity, which hitherto had been thought to be separate cognitive skills. The formula is revealed here for the first time in a business publication:

$$E + M = C°$$

Can you work out what the symbols stand for?

Both memory and creativity are based on imagination and association. Thus, putting effort into developing your memory will simultaneously develop your creativity and vice versa. Therefore, the formula decodes to: energy + and into memory yields infinite creativity. Whenever you are practising or applying mnemonic techniques, you are at the same time practising and enhancing your powers of creativity.

Quick start: memory
Use imagination and association plus the following 12 steps:

Synaesthesia. This is a blending of the senses: sight; smell; hearing; taste; touch; and kinaesthesia (an awareness of your body and its movement).

Movement. In any mnemonic image, movement adds a huge range of possibilities for your brain to link to (make them three-dimensional).

Association. Whatever you want to memorise, make sure you associate it with something fixed in your mental environment.

Sexuality. We all have a good memory in this area, so use it!

Humour. Make your images funny and surreal!

Imagination. Albert Einstein said, 'Imagination is more important than knowledge. For knowledge is limited, whereas imagination embraces the entire world, stimulating progress, giving birth to evolution.' The more you apply your imagination to memory, the better your memory will be.

Number. Numbering adds specificity and efficiency to the principle of order and sequence.

Symbolism. Substituting a more meaningful image for an ordinary or boring image increases the probability of recall.

Colour. Where appropriate, and whenever possible, use the full range of the rainbow, to make your ideas more 'colourful' and memorable.

Order and/or Sequence. In combination with the other principles, order and/or sequence allow for much more immediate reference, and increase the brain's possibilities for 'random access'.

Positive images. In most instances, positive and pleasant images are better for memory purposes, because they make the brain want to return to them. The brain may block unpleasant, negative images.

Exaggeration. In all your images, exaggerate size, shape, colour and sound.

By practising regularly, you will find that your memory improves dramatically and you will also see the clear link between memory and creativity.

Speed reading and creativity
So, how does being able to read faster add to your creativity? Speed reading dovetails into Mind Mapping and memory in that, once you have acquired the skills to absorb information more quickly, you are even more able to identify

the critical issues and to make connections between ideas and concepts. Once again, this system involves using imagination and association, which generates ever more creativity.

Some people might worry that greater speed is gained at the cost of full comprehension. This is not the case. Because of the way your eye–brain system works, the astonishing fact is that the faster you read, the better your comprehension. The whole process means that you speed up in all aspects of your reading ability.

Quick start: speed reading

Reading is the individual's total interrelationship with symbolic information and is a process that takes place on many different levels at the same time. The following is an interesting exercise, which shows that you have the innate capacity to read using your peripheral vision as well as your central vision. By this means, you use all 260 million of your eye's light-receivers to communicate with and illuminate your brain. Now, select a page of text and place your finger under a word in the centre of the page. Keep your eyes focused on this word and, without moving them:

See how many words you can observe to either side of the central word.
See how many words you can make out clearly above and below the word you are pointing at.
See if you can tell whether there is a number at the top or the bottom of the page and, if so, what that number is.
See whether you can count the number of paragraphs on the page.
See whether you can count the number of paragraphs on the opposite page.
Can you see a diagram on either of the pages?
If there is a diagram, can you determine clearly or roughly what it is illustrating?

By learning the speed reading techniques, you will be able to harness this peripheral vision and read with your brain and not just your eyes.

Every business needs to work creatively, and it is this creative edge that will deliver innovative ideas, products and concepts that give you the upper hand. I hope my quick-start introductions have given you practical insights into how this can be achieved.

Next, calculate your reading speed in words per minute (wpm) by dividing the number of words in the passage (in this case, 1825) by the time (in minutes) you took.

$$\text{Words per minute (wpm)} = \frac{\text{number of words}}{\text{time}}$$

When you have completed your calculation, enter the number in the wpm slot at the end of this paragraph and also enter it on your progress graph and chart on pages 222–3.

Words per minute: _____

Self-test 7: Comprehension

1 Mind Maps, memory, speed reading and information management make up what?
   (a) Imagination Toolkit for the Brain
   (b) Creativity Toolkit for the Brain
   (c) Study Skills Toolkit for the Brain
   (d) Mnemonic Toolkit for the Brain

2 Who wrote *The Road Ahead*?
   (a) Steve Jobs
   (b) M. Scott Peck
   (c) Bill Gates
   (d) Carl Sagan

3 According to the *Newsweek* article, what does creating a Mind Map entail?
   (a) Left-brain thinking
   (b) Whole-brain thinking
   (c) Right-brain thinking
   (d) Full mind set thinking

4   In the same article, creating a Mind Map is like playing:
    (a)   Table tennis
    (b)   A pinball machine
    (c)   Scrabble
    (d)   Chess

5   What is Tony Buzan's new creativity formula?
    (a) $E = MC^2$
    (b) $E + M = C°$
    (c) $M = E + C°$
    (d) $½ M = 2.5 E + M$

6   Kinaesthesia is a blending of the senses: sight, smell,
    hearing, taste and touch.   True/False

7   How many steps does Tony Buzan recommend for harnessing
    imagination and association?
    (a)   15
    (b)   10
    (c)   12
    (d)   7

8   Thomas Edison said, 'Imagination is more important
    than knowledge'.   True/False

9   Your eye has how many light-receivers?
    (a)   520 million
    (b)   260 million
    (c)   150 million
    (d)   1000 million

10 What generates more creativity? _____ and _____

Check your answers against those on page 217. Then divide your score by
10 and multiply by 100 to calculate your percentage comprehension.

                    Comprehension score: _____ out of 10

                                         _____ per cent

Now enter your score on your progress graph and chart on pages 222–3.

Conclusion: speeding into the future

Congratulations! You're near the end of the first stage in mastering the art of speed reading – the completion of this book. The next stages will include your subsequent reviews of the book, your continuing practice of the new skills you have discovered, and your delving into Mind Maps and other mnemonic devices.

You now possess all the basic knowledge about your eyes, your brain, about range and speed reading techniques, and how to mastermind your vocabulary. You are therefore fully armed to recognise, assimilate, comprehend and understand what you read, making appropriate connections, analysing, criticising, appreciating, selecting and rejecting. You are also fully primed to retain and recall information and finally to express and communicate the word as you see fit.

Your continuing success in all fields of speed reading depends on your personal decision to keep exploring the vast capacity of your brain to read, assimilate, comprehend, recall, communicate and create – an infinite capacity. Good luck!

Appendix 1: Self-test answers

The following pages provide the answers to the series of progressive tests and visual gulp exercises, and your self-completion graph and chart to monitor your speed reading speeds and progress. You will also find a helpful list of 'mind sport' websites, including a speed reading site if you wish to take your new-found skill further into the competitive level.

Self-test 1

1   False
2   (c)
3   (b)
4   True
5   (d)
6   (a)
7   (b)
8   (b)
9   (c)
10 (a)
11 (c)
12 (c)
13 False
14 (a)
15 (d)

Self-test 2

1   (c)
2   (b)
3   True
4   (b)
5   (c)
6   (a)
7   (b)
8   (c)
9   True
10 (c)
11 True
12 (b)
13 (b)
14 False

Self-test 3

1 (a)
2 False
3 (b)
4 (c)
5 (d)
6 Pod
7 (c)
8 (c)
9 (b)
10 (d)
11 False
12 (b)
13 (c)
14 False
15 (c)

Self-test 4

1 (b)
2 (c)
3 False
4 (d)
5 (a)
6 (c)
7 True

8 (c)
9 (d)
10 (d)
11 (a)
12 (c)
13 (b)
14 False
15 Human

Self-test 5

1 (b)
2 (b)
3 (c)
4 (c)
5 (c)
6 (b)
7 (b)
8 True
9 (d)
10 The mother's voice
11 (c)
12 False
13 (d)
14 (a)
15 (c)

Self-test 6

1 (a)
2 (c)
3 (c)
4 (b)
5 (b)
6 Rose bush
7 (d)
8 (a)
9 (b)
10 (d)
11 (b)
12 (c)
13 False
14 (d)
15 (c)

Self-test 7

1 (b)
2 (c)
3 (b)
4 (b)
5 (b)
6 True
7 (c)
8 False
9 (b)
10 Imagination and association

Appendix 2: vocabulary exercise answers

Exercise 1 (a)

1 (l)
2 (e)
3 (m)
4 (f)
5 (n)
6 (g)
7 (o)
8 (d)
9 (k)
10 (c)
11 (j)
12 (b)
13 (i)
14 (a)
15 (h)

Exercise 1 (b)

1 (e)
2 (i)
3 (d)
4 (n)
5 (j)
6 (f)
7 (k)
8 (c)
9 (a)
10 (l)
11 (g)
12 (o)
13 (m)
14 (h)
15 (b)

Exercise 1 (c)

1 (h)
2 (a)
3 (o)
4 (b)
5 (k)

6 (c)

7 (n)

8 (d)

9 (l)

10 (m)

11 (g)

12 (j)

13 (f)

14 (i)

15 (e)

Exercise 2 (a)

1 (f)

2 (l)

3 (k)

4 (i)

5 (e)

6 (h)

7 (d)

8 (n)

9 (m)

10 (a)

11 (j)

12 (b)

13 (g)

14 (c)

15 (o)

Exercise 2 (b)

1 (o)

2 (h)

3 (a)

4 (b)

5 (m)

6 (n)

7 (e)

8 (d)

9 (j)

10 (f)

11 (g)

12 (k)

13 (i)

14 (l)

15 (c)

Exercise 2 (c)

1 (o)

2 (f)

3 (c)

4 (n)

5 (m)

6 (i)

7 (k)

8 (a)

9   (j)

10   (l)

11   (b)

12   (e)

13   (g)

14   (d)

15   (h)

Exercise 3 (a)

1   (h)

2   (d)

3   (b)

4   (l)

5   (e)

6   (n)

7   (a)

8   (j)

9   (m)

10   (o)

11   (g)

12   (i)

13   (c)

14   (k)

15   (f)

Exercise 3 (b)

1   (d)

1   (a)

3   (k)

4   (h)

5   (j)

6   (l)

7   (n)

8   (m)

9   (o)

10   (b)

11   (g)

12   (f)

13   (c)

14   (e)

15   (i)

Exercise 3 (c)

1   (e)

2   (k)

3   (d)

4   (l)

5   (a)

6   (o)

7   (i)

8	(n)	12	(b)
9	(m)	13	(c)
10	(j)	14	(f)
11	(g)	15	(h)

Appendix 3: Progress graph

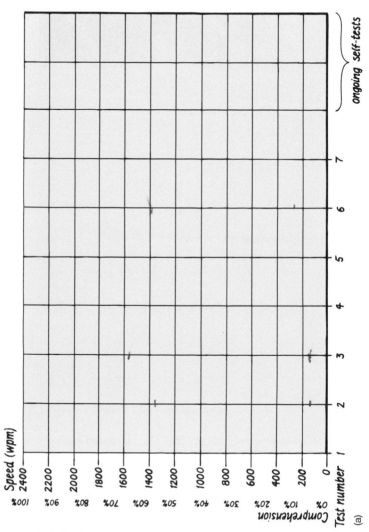

(a) Progress graph.

Progress chart

Reading number	Time (minute-second)	Speed (wpm)	Comprehension (%)
1			
2			
3			
4			
5			
6			
7			
8			
9			
10			

(b) Progress chart: ideally, use one colour for your speed reading and another colour for your comprehension

Appendix 4: Tony Buzan's Festival of the Mind online resources

The World Speed Reading Council was established to promote, train and recognise achievements in the field of speed reading worldwide. Apart from developing the ability to gain an understanding of large quantities of text in a short time, speed reading is one of the five learning mind sports that can be practised competitively. Their website is **www.worldspeedreadingcouncil.com**.

The Festival of the Mind is a showcase event for the five learning mind sports of memory, speed reading, IQ, creativity and Mind Mapping.

To aid you in your search for relevant speed reading, memory, mind sports and other brain training stimuli, here are the current websites associated with Tony Buzan and his Festival of the Mind – with explanatory reference.

The first Festival of the Mind was held in the Royal Albert Hall in 1995 and was organised by Tony Buzan and Raymond Keene OBE. Since then, the festival has been held in the UK, alongside the World Memory Championships in Oxford, and in other countries around the world, including Malaysia, China and Bahrain. Public interest in the five learning mind sports is growing worldwide, so, not surprisingly, the festival is a big attraction. An event devoted solely to Mind Maps with Tony Buzan filled the Albert Hall again in 2006.

Each of the mind sports has its own council to promote, administer and recognise achievement in its field.

 The World Memory Championships is the pre-eminent national and international memory competition, where records are continuously smashed. In the 2007 UK Memory Championships, Ben Pridmore memorised a single shuffled deck of playing cards in 26.28 seconds, beating the previous world record of 31.16 seconds set by Andi Bell. (For years, memorising a pack of cards in under 30 seconds had been seen as the memory equivalent of beating the four-minute mile in athletics.) Full details of the World Memory Championships can be found on the website **www.worldmemorychampionships.com**. Its interactive Mind Map was designed by Mind Map World Champion Phil Chambers using Buzan's iMind Map.

 Since it was founded in 1991, the World Memory Championships has created a gold standard for memory based on ten different memory disciplines. A simplified version of these has now been created specifically for schools memory competitions, backed up with a training programme to help teachers to train memory techniques.

In a nationwide educational partnership, consisting of the UK Memory Sports Council, Inspire Education and national government initiative Aimhigher, students are taught powerful memory techniques that, when put into practice, can provide the intellectual platform for recalling almost anything, instantly. These techniques are being passed on to teachers and pupils at secondary schools throughout the UK by means of the UK Schools Memory Championships.

Organised by Inspire Education and spearheaded by eight times World Memory Champion Dominic O'Brien and Chief Arbiter of the World Memory Championships Phil Chambers, the UK Schools

Memory Competition has been created to help pupils discover the mind sport of memory and to develop their mental skills to help their studies. We are in the process of creating a model in the UK that can be repeated around the world, with the goal of eventually establishing the World Schools Memory Championships soon after 2010. For more information, log on to **www.schoolsmemorychampionships.com**.

 Welcome to Tony Buzan's world. Tony Buzan is the inventor of Mind Maps – the most powerful thinking tool of our times. Discover more about Tony and the transformative powers of Mind Mapping, Memory and Speed Reading at **www.buzanworld.com**.

 The WorldwideBrain Club, set up by the Buzan Organisation, encourages the formation of brain clubs worldwide. These have flourished for many years and bring together Mind Mapping, creativity, IQ, speed reading and memory. Practising each of these disciplines positively impacts on the others. Using Mind Maps, for example, helps with creativity, as it presents ideas in a brain-friendly way that inspires new ideas. Working on memory techniques makes the brain more capable in every other area, in the same way that working out in a gym builds muscles.

Brain Clubs, whether set up in a school or college, or within an organisation or company, create a supportive environment where all their members share the same objective – to give their personal 'neck-top computer' the best operating system possible. Buzan Centres Worldwide provide qualified trainers in all of these areas. See **www.buzanworld.com** and **www.worldbrainclub.com**.

The Brain Trust is a registered charity founded in 1990 by Tony Buzan with one objective: to maximise the ability of each and every individual to unlock and deploy the vast capacity of his or her brain. Its charter includes promoting research into the study of thought processes and the investigation of the mechanics of thinking, manifested in learning, understanding, communication, problem-solving, creativity and decision-making. In 2008 Professor Baroness Susan Greenfield won its Brain of the Century award. Visit **www.braintrust.org.uk**.

The International Academy of Mental World Records at **www.mentalworldrecords .com** exists to recognise the achievements of mental athletes around the world. In addition to arbiting world record attempts and awarding certificates of achievement, the Academy is also linked to the International Festival of the Mind, which showcases mental achievements in the five learning mind sports of memory, speed reading, creativity, Mind Mapping and IQ.

Creativity is defined by Torrance, the doyen of creativity testing, as follows:

Creativity is a process of becoming sensitive to problems, deficiencies, gaps in knowledge, missing elements, disharmonies and so on; identifying the difficulty; searching for solutions; making guesses or formulating hypotheses about the deficiencies; testing and re-testing these hypotheses and possibly modifying and retesting them; and finally communicating the results.

Creativity is one of the five learning mind sports along with Mind Mapping, speed reading, IQ and memory.

All of these skills positively impact on the others and together they can help any individual to be more effective in whatever they choose to do. All five learning mind sports are featured in the Festival of the Mind. Visit **www.worldcreativitycouncil.com**.

Intelligence quotient (IQ) is one of the five learning mind sports, which include Mind Mapping, creativity, speed reading and memory. The website of the World IQ Council can be found at **www.worldiqcouncil.com**. You can test your IQ on this site.

The World Memory Sports Council is the independent governing body of the mind sport of memory and regulates competitions worldwide. Tony Buzan is the president of the Council. You can visit the website at **www.worldmemorysportscouncil.com**.

Mind Mapping is a 'thought organisation technique' invented by the international author and expert on the brain, Tony Buzan, in 1971. The World Mind Mapping Council administers and promotes the sport and also awards the prestigious title of Mind Mapping World Champion. The current reigning world champion is Phil Chambers. Visit the website at **www.worldmindmappingcouncil.com**.

Index

Page numbers in *italics* denotes a diagram/table

Unleash the power of your mind with these bestselling titles from the world's leading authority on the brain and learning...

The Mind Map Book
Unlock your creativity, boost your memory, change your life
Tony Buzan

9781406647167

The original and the best book on Mind Maps from their world-renowned inventor.

The Memory Book
Boost your memory, year after year
Tony Buzan

781406644265

Embark on the most exciting intellectual adventure of your life and discover how easy it is to supercharge your memory.

Mind Maps for Business
Revolutionise your business thinking and practice
Tony Buzan
and Chris Griffiths

*81406642902

Unlock the power of your brain to transform your business practice and performance with the ultimate 21st Century business tool – the Mind Map.